"Seeing is believing"

For Nick, Lucas, Lola, Felix and Tia X

Ko Papatūānuku au, me taku moko Kahuku! Anei i roto hei kōrero ki tō tātou Iwi

Mother Earth and her grandchild the butterfly have a message for all people!

An Educational Guide on Monarch Butterflies

"Nothing excites me more than witnessing children in the outdoors, observing nature and its beauty, the joy it brings children studying these creatures is magnificent".

"Forgotten are the struggles that a caterpillar has today, as tomorrow a magnificent change will occur and a butterfly will appear and you will see the beauty of life once again".

In memory of our beloved beagle Tia R.I.P

Acknowledgements

To Mitre 10 Mega Canterbury for their support in the early days with my first edition. Especially Peter Grenfell and Josh Tasker from the Papanui store who believed in me and were so sincere and lovely to deal with. I couldn't have found a better group of people to partner with at the start of my journey. Mitre 10 Mega Canterbury made my dream of publishing my first book come true. And for that, you have my deep gratitude.

Book cover designed by my clever friend Sigrid Jokschus.

Butterfly Musketeers logo and children butterfly colouring template designed by my friend Denise Manns of Sacred Geometry Queenstown.

Edited by Fran Pashby.

All photography by Maria Romero including front cover photos, unless stated otherwise.

logo on discussions in the classroom page Copyright: canaryluc 123RF Stock Photo
logos on monarch activities & poems pages Copyright: thawats 123RF Stock Photo
logo on science project page Copyright: kerstiny 123RF Stock Photo
logo on North American migrating page Copyright: sunshinesmile 123RF Stock Photo
logo on FAQ & glossary pages, how can we help save the monarchs Copyright: lightwise123RF Stock Photo
triple Monarch logo on word search answers Copyright: sunshinesmile 123RF Stock Photo
triple monarchs on contents page Copyright : Thawat Tanhai 123RF Stock Photo
Back cover photo Konrad Kreative
Caterpillar and Chrysalis Anatomy Irina Alex

Although the author has made every effort to ensure that the information in this book was correct at publication, the author does not assume and hereby disclaims any liability to any party for any loss, damage, or disruption caused by errors or omissions, whether such errors or omissions result from negligence, accident, or any other cause.

To order more copies please visit www.thebutterflymusketeers.com

Also available at any Canterbury Mitre10 stores

1st edition printed Dec 2016
2nd edition printed Nov 2017
3rd edition printed Aug 2019

ISBN 978-0-473-41455-9

National Library of New Zealand Cataloging in Publication Data

Acknowledgements

When I was writing the first edition of my first book, it never once crossed my mind that I was going to become an author at the end of it. My mission was purely to get my message out there to educate and teach people how to care for the monarch butterflies correctly. It was never about fame or fortune. I wanted to share the sheer enjoyment and sense of fulfilment that I get from caring for monarch butterflies that share our planet.

Months after launching my first book, I was thinking "what next after my book? How could I expand my teachings?" But after a short break, I quickly decided this was my sole purpose. I finally know that my passion is to build an awareness of the monarch butterflies and encourage their conservation through education. I own my purpose now, and it's a pleasure to be able to put together this third edition of " An Educational Guide on Monarch Butterflies".

It's amazing to share and see people raising caterpillars. I am committed now and have so many wonderful visions to share for the future with you. Butterflies are creatures of hope, the caterpillar reminds us that humans also have struggles but once a caterpillar ends, it teaches us that something new and beautiful is about to be born. As humans, butterflies teach us so much on a spiritual level, that we can fly high and achieve the most impossible dreams imagined. That we all have struggles like the caterpillar, doing mundane things each day, not knowing what tomorrow may bring us. We too can turn into a chrysalis by looking within, being still, finding answers ourselves and learning about our true self, so we can transform into a better person. I hope you enjoy reading this latest edition of my book, and that it enables you to contribute to the conservation and continued survival of the monarch butterfly in New Zealand.

****

The love and support of my husband Nick and children Lucas, Lola and Felix who let me vanish for hours on end in the garden taking care of the caterpillars, sorting out my swan plants, taking photos or just watching them and researching for the guide book. I'm so grateful you are by my side helping and caring for the monarchs, sharing my interest and passion too.

With the help of many empowering loving friends around me that give me that courage, support and make me shine my light to others, this is for you.

To all the people that breed monarch butterflies, that do a great job all summer long caring for the caterpillars and buying endless amounts of swan plants for their caterpillars.

For my daughter's teacher, Sam Jones, who inspired me. Having observed my daughter's artwork on monarchs in her classroom, I offered to write a short two page guide for the class who were actively learning about the life cycle. Now this small guide is more than I could have ever imagined. During writing this guide and speaking to people, I have discovered that there is a need for a guide for the next generation of children and teachers to educate, care for and save the monarch butterflies.

To my wonderful friend Fran Pashby; I will be forever in your gratitude. I loved the way you were able to read my mind and re-write this book. You are so talented, you came at the perfect time, so willingly and I couldn't have done it without you.

Lastly to all the monarch butterflies that follow and flutter around me on my walks, hang around my garden on a summer's day and put a smile on my face whenever or wherever I see them.

Foreword

This book is about the magic of butterflies. Butterflies lift our spirit, engage with our happy memories, remind us of the amazing diversity of life on Earth and make us long for freedom. I was captured by this butterfly magic from an early age.

For most people monarchs epitomise summertime and the freedom of school holidays and annual leave. Their size, colour and gliding flight allow them to not only be visible to lots of people in our cities and towns, but for us to follow their flight and inspire us with their beauty.

I have been enchanted by butterflies and moths since I was a small boy growing up in Invercargill. I still have my hand-written notes and sketches from the time I decided on 15 November 1969 that I would study them for the rest of my life. Now 48 years later I have a computerised diary of the 3,474 expeditions that I have carried out since then in the pursuit of them. This wonderful journey of exploration and discovery has taken me to remote mountain tops, inland salt pans, rocky places and dry grasslands, coastal beaches and bluffs nationwide to find our gorgeous butterflies and moths. Along the way I have had the thrill of discovering over 150 new species and better understanding the ecology and specialised life histories of our 2,000 plus species of butterflies and moths. I am still fascinated by the close association our moths and butterflies have with our native plants growing in particular habitats. I still love the challenge of detailed observations to record and describe these associations.

It has been an incredible journey of surprises too. I have found that we have 62 species of butterfly that naturally live here or visit our shores after incredible journeys over the vast Pacific Ocean. These long distance migrants include the monarch, and we continue to record new migrants such as the blue triangle as recently as March 2017 in Christchurch. Working with my son Hamish and examining closely the DNA and morphology of our butterflies, we believe that 46 of this total are endemic to New Zealand.

When I worked as Collections and Research Manager at the Otago Museum I came up with the idea of adding a Tropical butterfly enclosure to the Discovery World Science Centre in the museum. I led the team that researched, planned and built it, opening in 2007. I was fortunate too as I got to travel overseas to not only visit other indoor tropical butterfly houses to get ideas for our one, but also to the tropical countries where they breed the butterflies and supply the museum with chrysalises from which the butterflies emerge.

I have promoted butterflies and moths on stamps and our banknotes too. New Zealand Post produced a beautiful issue of butterflies in 1995 and I helped them with a Pacific issue of butterflies too. The South Island zebra moth on our $100 banknote was my idea and after some discussion I got them to make it bigger and brighter on the new version of the notes recently!

I know you'll enjoy Maria's book as much as I did. Her effectiveness in environmental education is truly inspirational and infectious. And enjoy the monarch butterflies as much as Maria and I do too!

Brian Patrick
Senior Ecologist and Entomologist

Contents Page

3	Tia
4	Acknowledgments (and p5)
6	Foreword by Brian Patrick
8	Introduction
9	The beautiful monarch butterfly
10	Building your butterfly friendly garden
11	How to attract butterflies to your garden
12	Milkweed plants (swan plants)
13	Caring for your plants and seed pods over winter
14	Life cycle (Metamorphosis)
15	Monarch anatomy
16	The Good and the Bad - Chrysalis
17	The caterpillar stage & Handling your caterpillars
18	Changing to a chrysalis
19	The monarch emerges
20	How to differentiate between male and female monarchs
21	The five instar stages
22	Frequently asked questions (and p23)
24	What do the children learn? (and p25)
26	Overwintering sites in New Zealand (and p27)
28	Threats to monarch butterflies
29	How can we help save the monarch butterflies?
30	North American migrating (and p31)
32	Taking care of your chrysalides
33	How to combat aphids
34	The Butterfly Musketeers (and p35)
36	My observations of autumn monarchs (and p37)
38	Diseases that occur when breeding monarchs (and p39)
40	Butterfly life cycle word search
41	Discussion questions for the classroom
42	18 Fun facts
43	Butterfly colouring template
44	Butterfly poems
45	Science questions on monarchs
46	Monarchs in the classroom; Activities (and p47)
48	Imperfections
49	Yates NZ How to sow swan plants from seed
50	Further information
51	Word search answers
52	Glossary (and p53)
54	St James Park

Introduction

The purpose of this educational guide is to give you, the reader, a deeper understanding and an awareness of how unique monarch butterflies are to our planet. To give you access to detailed information on how to look after monarchs during every stage of their lives, plus raise awareness on the issues that arise from diseases and predators. The guide is an excellent resource for teachers working in pre-schools or primary schools, who want to learn more to teach their students; or perhaps you are that person like me, who treats their caterpillars as pets, and rushes out to the garden centre for emergency supplies of swan plants. Monarchs have become my true passion in life and now I want to share that, so that together we can attempt to save the monarch butterfly from extinction.

I first discovered swan plants at a Playcentre in 2010. I was as amazed and enthralled as my children were, and thought how fantastic it was that anyone could buy a swan plant and watch the beautiful process of metamorphosis take place in their own home or garden. Every year, I bought more and more swan plants. My hobby grew alongside my interest and knowledge, and before long my children took over the care of the plants and their special creatures. My children always made sure there were enough leaves for the caterpillars to feed on, and counted each day how many chrysalises there were, always noticing when a monarch was about to emerge.

This guide will also help you to understand the different types of diseases which can occur, and advise you on the best methods of prevention. It will teach you the importance of hygiene around the plants and animals, and explain the signs of possibly sick caterpillars and butterflies. When I first became interested in monarchs, I had no idea why some would emerge from their chrysalises weak or disfigured, but having completed an online course in Butterfly Gardening, and more importantly studying the whole process in my own back garden for many years. I have much more of an understanding that I aim to share with you. There is so much hearsay information around about feeding caterpillars pumpkin. That swan plants are toxic, so they aren't allowed in school. Yes, it's true but once we are educated about them and the necessary precautions are in place it's ok to have them in schools. I want to share some light on these two major areas that I get asked about constantly. It's all about the education and awareness

In the beginning, I never knew that when a caterpillar wandered away from its host plant and hung itself face down on another plant or pot rim, that it was getting ready to moult. This is when a caterpillar leaves the food source, makes a mat of silk and sheds its skin, revealing a new bright skin beneath. The old dead skin is abandoned (or occasionally eaten, if its a VERY hungry caterpillar!), and the caterpillar returns to its original host plant to carry on chomping. I spent many hours picking up caterpillars and putting them back on the plants they had just left. I wish I'd known then what I know now! It's so important at this time NOT to disturb them. Moving them from their silk mat will make it harder, if not impossible for them to successfully moult, and it can cause issues and tear their prolegs. If you must put a caterpillar back on a leaf, make sure your other hand is underneath for a few seconds until you are sure they have gripped on tight.

Having a lot of swan plants is wonderful, but also increases the risk of diseases spreading. It only takes one infected monarch to lay eggs on a swan plant for the whole batch to potentially become infected. Other challenges include predators such as wasps stinging caterpillars, and birds and spiders eating adult monarchs. However, the deadliest predator is the parasite/spore, OE, which cannot even be seen with the human eye. This is one very good reason to keep your plants clear of frass (caterpillar poop), and to disinfect your plants carefully between each 'batch' of caterpillars.

I aim to share everything I have experienced over the years as a monarch lover, to give you a better understanding of how to raise these glorious creatures and enjoy a wonderful garden full of flowers and dancing butterflies. A butterfly garden will give you the chance to explore nature with your camera and take great photos of caterpillars, monarchs, flowers and chrysalises. Observing a monarch butterfly as it transforms from a caterpillar to a chrysalis to a butterfly, is amongst the most thrilling experiences nature has to offer, and a true phenomenon.

The beautiful monarch butterfly

There are over 20,000 known species of butterfly around the world. The most popular here in New Zealand is the monarch butterfly. *Danaus plexippus* is its scientific name. Originally from North America, the monarch butterfly is considered a native species having established itself in New Zealand in the 1870s, and has now become one of our national icons. The average monarch butterfly weighs under one gram and their wingspan is just over 10 cms. Monarch butterflies have an important role as pollinators of many plants. Their Māori name is Kakahu.

Butterflies live on every continent on earth except Antartica, and the majority are found in tropical rainforests. They have also been to space in 2009 as an educational experiment on board a space station with astronauts. Their habitats range from dry deserts to swampy marshes and luckily for us, local parks and in our own back gardens. The monarch butterflies have also established themselves in Hawaii, Samoa and Tahiti, as well as Australia, transported by ship or carried by the wind. The largest population is located in Southern Canada and Northern United States, from where the monarchs migrate every year to Mexico for winter. Most adult monarchs are herbivores, meaning they have a plant diet. They use their proboscis (long curly tubular mouth part) to suck in nectar from flowers, and water. The larvae of monarchs are called caterpillars. Their job is to eat, grow, store food and develop into chrysalises. Caterpillars are bright yellow, black and white to warn predators that they might be poisonous to eat. Monarchs are cold blooded which means they cannot make heat inside their bodies and they need sunlight to warm themselves up and fly.

The female monarch lays eggs by curling up her abdomen and laying eggs on the under side of the leaves of the swan plant. Each egg, which is the size of a pin head, will then take between five and 12 days to hatch, depending on what part of New Zealand you live in. The eggs are stuck on with their own special glue. Once the caterpillar has hatched, it will eat its own egg shell for protein, then heads onto the tender new leaves at the very top of the swan plant.

Building your butterfly friendly garden

If you're going to raise monarchs, you're going to need lots of swan plants. Swan plants are a type of milkweed and are the only plant a caterpillar will eat and lay eggs on, because of this I consider this plant pretty special. Before you start planting, you need to plan where would be the ideal spot in your garden for your butterfly area. The monarchs, caterpillars and chrysalises should be protected from the wind and have some shade, with plenty of afternoon sun. To attract monarchs to your garden, you will need lots of wild flowers for the butterflies to feed off the nectar. Plant your swan plants close to your flowers so the butterflies can be near nectar plants, mixing them up, creating shelter for your caterpillars. You can buy cheap punnets of flowers (that are great for butterfly gardens) at school fairs and garden centres.   Add more flowers every month if you can.   Make sure you constantly deadhead the dead flowers as this will produce more flowers and your plants will bloom longer. Wild flower seeds from packets are very easy for children to grow, you can scatter the seeds in hanging baskets or on your soil and a variety of flowers will soon appear.

The monarchs will love them, plus you will be caring for the wonderful bees that pollinate the flowers too. Flowers are a valuable nectar source for pollinators. You will have a great, bright looking garden full of colour to admire and relax in. Once you have a nectar-rich garden, the monarchs will be sure to follow and feed, and lay eggs on your swan plants.   When you buy swan plants, make sure they are sturdy with plenty of leaves. You should have only a few eggs on each plant otherwise the plants will be striped of leaves very quickly by the hungry caterpillars. It's cruel, but I'd rather crush a few eggs on my swan plants with my fingers at this stage than see caterpillars starve later on. I would recommend a maximum of four or five eggs on an average sized swan plant to start with, then replacing your swan plant with another one just before the plant gets totally eaten.

The following flowers are ideal ones to purchase or grow from seed in your garden, both for the monarchs and for yourself to enjoy. Cosmos, Sunflowers, Echinaceas, Rudbeckias, Zinneas and Azaleas are rich in nectar and are great to have in your garden. Buddleia bushes are butterflies absolute favourite flower and they are attracted to Petunias too. I particularly recommend Marigold flowers, as they are great to repel aphids and will help save your swan plants from being attacked. Spring flowers such as Verbena and Cineraria are vital for butterflies coming out of overwintering, hungry for nectar. Nasturtiums are among the easiest of flowers to grow from seed. The seeds are the size of a pea and they can be planted straight into the earth. Be aware Nasturtiums spread and grow rapidly and self seed, so sow the seed in a large space. These can be sown four weeks before the last winter frost. During the summer months Nasturtiums can be cut back and the flower or leaves can also be eaten, or used as decoration in salads.

Watering is best in the morning or evening, as during the day the water will just evaporate and burn the flowering leaves. Also that way you are helping to conserve water.

Right photo: My then 10 month old Felix already getting involved in our butterfly garden, not fazed about a new little monarch butterfly on his head.

How to attract butterflies to your garden

- Sow or purchase swan plants, it's that simple and is vital for the monarch population to breed. Plant the swan plants in a few areas in your garden. Plan ahead and make sure you have heaps of swan plants so you never run out. Put some swan plants to one side, and cover them up. Let them grow bushy before exposing them to the monarchs. If you love the red or yellow admiral butterflies, stinging nettles will attract them into your garden as they are the host plant for the admiral caterpillars.

- Butterflies love bright colours so plant the right colours. Plant red, yellow, orange, pink and purple nectar flowers, especially Zinnas and Cosmos which the Monarchs Butterflies love.

- Butterflies typically only feed in full sun so make sure you plant your nectar flowers in full sunshine. Also make sure this planting is sheltered from the wind.

- Avoid insecticides because they kill insects. Go organic. Spraying toxic sprays disturbs the natural organisms in your soil, and risks disrupting the natural ecosystem of your garden, not to mention the risks they pose to our own health.

- Provide shelter. Butterflies, bees and other pollinators need shelter to hide from predators. Let a pile of grass cuttings or a log decompose in a sunny place on the ground. Allow a dead tree to stand to create nooks for butterflies and solitary bees.

- Butterflies are attracted to muddy puddles which they will flock to for salts and nutrients as well as water. Bees, birds and butterflies also all need water, so having a birdbath somewhere to catch the rain is a really good idea.

- Even if you have a very small garden or courtyard you can still do your bit to attract the bees and butterflies by having one or two hanging baskets or a plant pot with a few nectar flowers in it.

- Dedicate an area or patch of your lawn not to be cut and let the grass grow and sprinkle wild flower seeds. This will grow into a meadow and is great for the birds too. Plus nicer on the eye as it will be a patch of colours and flowers. A pollinator paradise for sure!

Milkweed plants (swan plants)

Swan plants are part of the milkweed family, also known as *Asclepiadaceae*, which is a host plant for the monarchs to lay their eggs on. Swan plants are easily accessible in most major garden centres from September to March, although at times there are places that simply cannot meet demand and sell out. A swan plant is a perennial. If cared for correctly with good nutritional soil and regular plant food, it can live for many years.

There is also another type of swan plant that the caterpillars eat here in New Zealand. It's a tropical milkweed plant also known as *Asclepias curassavica* or Silky Mix, plant. Seeds and plants are available in New Zealand. The plant has thicker leaves with a purple tinge, and produces bright beautiful yellow and red flowers that the tiny caterpillars like to hide in. This plant thrives in full sun, the flowers will be a great source of nectar for the pollinators (see picture insert on next page).

"Milkweed is poisonous when ingested, but it is not banned in schools and educational institutions in New Zealand because of its educational value in teaching young children about metamorphosis and as an introduction to scientific experimentation. The child would have to eat 10% of their body weight of the plant to get sick, it tastes extremely bitter"[1]. Although it's best to supervise, do not let your children touch the plant or caterpillars as this too can have an adverse effect, as children's hands can have traces of sunscreen and soap which are harmful to caterpillar skin. To avoid giving your caterpillars swan plants that have been sprayed with pesticide be sure you buy your plants from a reputable garden centre. Alternatively feed your caterpillars the plants that you have raised yourself from seed. That way your plants are free from any pesticides, insecticides or fertilisers, as monarchs tend to be very susceptible to poisoning.

All milkweed species contain cardenolides, which are nutrients inside the plant that help the caterpillar form a chrysalis. They are also toxic which is why children should never eat them, and also why the birds don't eat the monarch caterpillars! Always wash your hands immediately after handling swan plants, as you might wipe your eyes to get your hard-working sweat off and there may be traces of sap on your hands. The sap could also splatter from trimming the stalks. This can lead to blindness in the eye, so watch out for stinging in the eyes. Make sure you flush out with room-temperature water for at least 15 minutes and seek medical advice.

What can I do to minimise a child ingesting swan plant?

- Supervise children at all times when they are around the swan plants.
- Encourage children to enjoy the swan plant and butterflies without eating them.
- Grow swan plants in pots that can be removed to an area inaccessible to children when not being used.
- Alternatively place a netted fence around the swan plants, so it is unreachable to children without adult help. This is a great idea I've seen at Kids First Kindergartens.

Specific first aid advice for swan plant exposure; what should I do?

- **If swallowed** - Immediately seek medical advice from your poisons centre or your doctor. It is not necessary to give any fluids. Do not make the person vomit.
- **If on skin** - Immediately flush the exposed area with lots of water and seek medical advice from your poisons centre or your doctor
- **If in eyes** - Flush the eye with room-temperature water for at least 15 minutes and seek medical advice from your poisons centre or your doctor

Swan plants are not on the Landcare Research list "Safety in pre-school centres: plants to avoid," although they are on the "plants in New Zealand poisonous to children" list. With the correct systems in place to supervise your children and by educating the kids on the potential dangers of swan plants, the benefits outweigh the slight risk, in the unlikely event of the milky sap being ingested by a child.

---

[1]Information regarding swan plants when ingested, first aid and what to do sourced from - *Poison Prevention and Education New Zealand* www.poisons.co.nz

Caring for your plants over Winter

During winter months I would recommend gathering up all your swan plants that are in pots and placing them in your greenhouse or a friend's greenhouse if you haven't got one. If they are in the ground, place a frost cloth around the plant and cover the base. Then add pea straw around the soil to protect the roots from freezing and killing the plant. Remember to water your plants throughout the winter months.

Before covering or moving your swan plants, trim back brown stems, as this aids regrowth. If you have swan plants that are just stalks make sure you take care of them by frequent watering, plus feeding them with Yates Thrive natural seaweed tonic. This reduces transplant shock in new plants, aids recovery from stress conditions, and improves plant resistance, (against heat, frost, drought, pests and diseases). I also add in some sheep pellets (which can be purchased from any garden centre) deep below the roots in the new pots. Sheep pellets help stimulate green growth and enhance the leaves to grow back quicker. You can also snip back any stems that are not healthy looking and brown. These plants will soon be ready for another round of caterpillars in the following season. Please ensure that you wash your hands throughly after you have been touching swan plants. Be aware that when trimming your swan plants, milk sap from the plants could spurt into your eye which can cause stinging and harm.

Caring for your seed pods

A great idea is to cover all seed pods with organza bags, which you can purchase from a $2 shop, or buy online. Tie the bag over the entire seed pod when they are nearly ready, this will also stop the caterpillars from eating the pod (see photo below). The pod seeds will explode into the bag when mature and big. To separate the seeds simply empty them (together with the silky fluff) into a paper bag containing a few coins, shake - and the coins help to separate the seeds! Another alternative is when the pod is mature, open in half, hold one end of the silk and pull away - the seeds will slide off into the jar below. I found this an effective way of collecting seeds. You can then store the seeds in your refrigerator in a brown bag or an airtight glass jar. This simulates the period of dormancy the seeds need, before being planted into the soil in spring.

Left photo: Seed pods covered in organza bags. Right photo: Silky Mix flowers.

Life cycle (Metamorphosis)

A butterfly's life cycle is made up of four parts; egg, larva (caterpillar), pupa (chrysalis) and adult monarch. The word 'metamorphosis' comes from the Greek language "Meta" (meaning to change) and "Morphe" (meaning form, structure). Process of transformation from egg to adult is completed in about 30 days, depending largely on season and temperature.

Diagram courtesy of www.milkweedformonarchs.org

Average life span
- Egg 5-12 days
- Caterpillar 10-12 days
- Chrysalis 14-21 days
- Monarch: Approximately six weeks in the summer, longer in the winter, six to eight months

Monarch butterfly and caterpillar anatomies

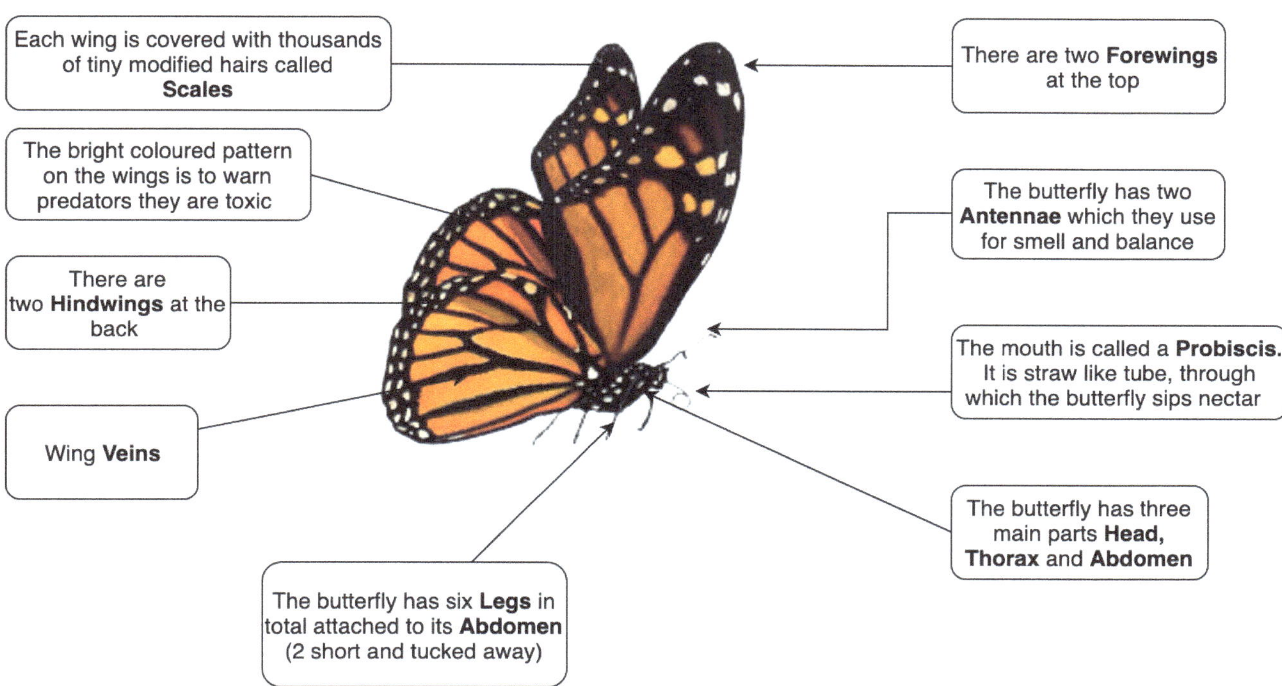

Caterpillar Anatomy

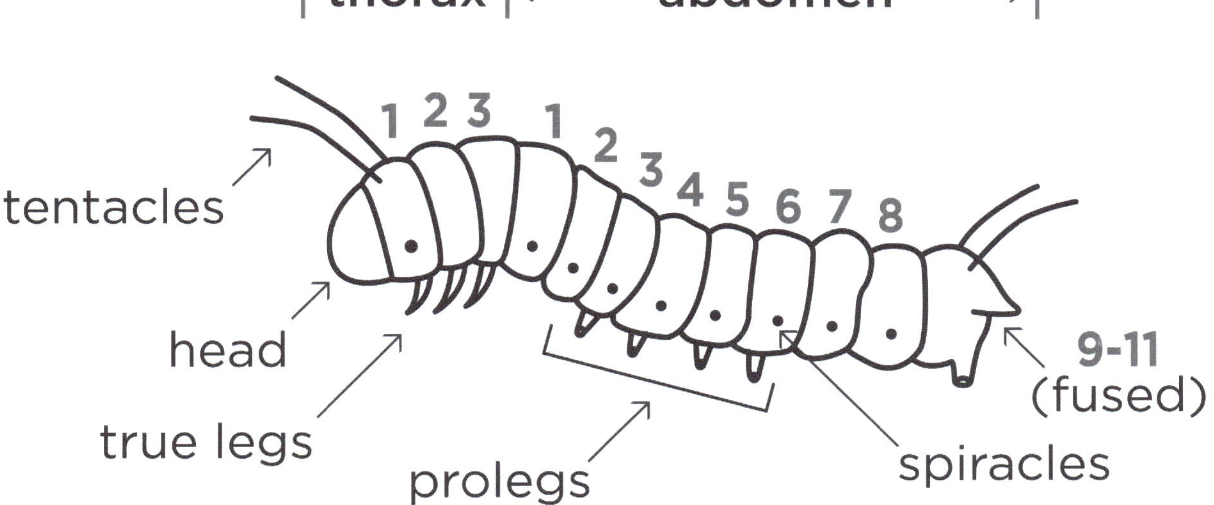

True Legs caterpillars have six legs emerging from their thorax
Tentacles are used as sensory organs. The caterpillar relies on its tentacles due to poor vision. They also have smaller tentacles at the back.
Spiracles are where they take in oxygen and breathe.
Prolegs, attached to their abdomen, enable them to crawl along and grip whilst vertical.

The Good and the Bad - Chrysalis

A common question I get asked is about chrysalides, and how to tell if they are good or bad (alive or dead). With healthy chrysalides, you will notice the wings of a monarch will stay an emerald green colour until a couple of days before emergence begins. The rule of thumb is that it shouldn't be black for more than 3 days. If it is, it's likely the monarch inside the chrysalis is diseased, or a predator has laid its eggs inside and killed the chrysalis. If the chrysalis has been very dark for at least five days and you cannot see the orange wings through the transparent casing, the monarch butterfly inside is dead and it will then dry up. Dispose of your dead chrysalis to avoid disease spreading. If you are in a part of the country that is prone to Asian Paper Wasps, it's a good idea to bring your chrysalides into a safe space indoors or invest in a caterpillar castle. I love these as the caterpillars are safe and often I find it amazing when I see them congregating in the same corner, hanging in J positions. Perhaps it's like safety in numbers or they just have the sheep mentality and follow the leader!

To remove the chrysalis you start by pulling the silk around the top of the cremaster and then gentle move it and hang it up. You can also tie string around the cremaster then hang the string with tape on a shelf for the Monarch to emerge safely.   I would also remove the chrysalides that are hanging on the leaves of the milkweed, especially if other caterpillars are still eating the plant, as this will avoid the chrysalis accidentally crashing down. Always make sure the emerging butterfly has enough room to dry its wings properly.

Moving chrysalises isn't difficult, but it definitely takes practise. As colder weather arrives in autumn chrysalides take a lot longer than normal to emerge into a butterfly. The chances of a deformed butterfly emerging is higher, as throughout the summer bacteria have had time to build up on your plants.

The Good
The Bad

Chrysalis Anatomy

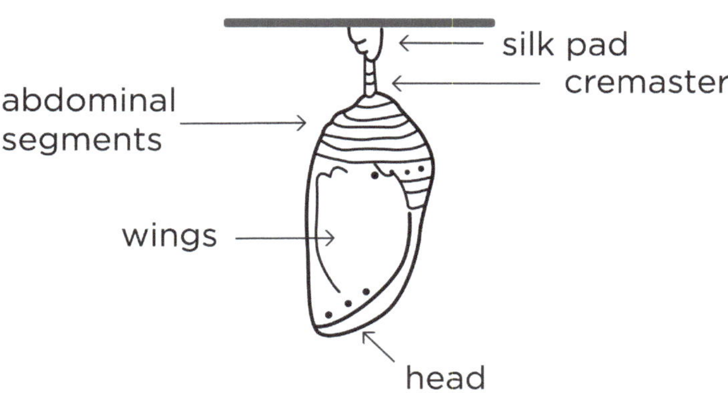

The caterpillar stage

It will take about five days for the eggs to hatch. The caterpillar's mission in life is to eat and grow, it will grow too big for its skin up to five times. It will take about two weeks for the caterpillars to reach full size. During that time, their development is very rapid. They increase in size 200 to 300 times. It is best not to handle the caterpillars while they are very small because they are fragile and may be injured. All you will need to do at this stage is to make sure there is plenty of food and that the swan plant is well watered and cleaned, because all the eating that the caterpillars do creates a lot of caterpillar poop! You may wish to put paper towels or a tray down to keep the area tidy and clean. When they are about 4.5 cm long, in the fifth instar, they will want to pupate and need to be able to climb so that they can hang in the 'J' shaped position and transform into a chrysalis. Fully grown caterpillars tend to wander and stop eating before they hang and change into a chrysalis. It is a good idea to contain them with a net covering to stop the wasps attacking at this stage.

Handling your caterpillars

Caterpillars are very susceptible to a variety of bacterial infections, including bacteria we all carry on our hands. Be sure to always wash your hands thoroughly before handling the caterpillars, as even sun lotion can kill them. Caterpillars are relatively fragile creatures, handle them VERY GENTLY. They can be killed if they are dropped even a very short height. When caterpillars walk, they may cling very tightly to the surface they are walking on. Never pull them off any surface (including your hands), because they will often hold so tightly that you can rip their prolegs off before they will let go. If you find a caterpillar that has wandered off from their plant, it's best to nudge their body to make sure it's not anchored for a moult. If you are changing them to another swan plant, it is best to put the fresh swan plant next to the old one for the caterpillars to crawl across on their own. Alternatively you can pick up the caterpillars with a clean paint brush and transfer them onto the new plant. Only move the caterpillars if there is nothing left but the stem with no leaves. The new plant must be well watered, as it may have high toxicity levels compared to the plant the caterpillar has just been eating from. You can also put them at the base of the plant, so they can crawl up the plant themselves. A caterpillar's job is just to eat and eat and eat, so the most important part of caring for a caterpillar is to provide a constant supply of fresh food. Caterpillars don't need to drink, they get all the hydration they need from their swan plant. The photo (above left) is not an ideal situation as there are too many caterpillars on one plant. Limit the amount of caterpillars you have on each plant, ensuring there's sufficient amount of space and leaves as a food source. Remember, the less we handle the caterpillars the better, it can actually kill them.

Changing to a chrysalis

Diagram courtesy of www.learnaboutnature.com

When the time comes to pupate, the caterpillars will find a sheltered, safe spot in which to transform into an adult and form their chrysalis (hard green case) which will protect them through this process. If your caterpillars are outside, they will usually hang from the roof of the cage or branch and turn into a chrysalis. They should be left in this position until the monarch emerges. Make sure your chrysalis is out of direct sunlight. The word 'chrysalis' comes from the Greek word for gold, and you can see an amazing line of gold dots around the top once the chrysalis is fully formed. This is the start of the process of metamorphosis. Chrysalises cannot fly, bite, sting or run away if discovered by a predator, they are completely helpless. One of the main reasons the chrysalis is green is to blend in with the surrounding environment.

What is the difference between a chrysalis and a cocoon?

This question will come up a lot and people do get confused until they read about it. The chrysalis is a butterfly pupa, which is a hard case which appears after the caterpillar's final shedding of its skin. It attaches to a leaf via a silk pad spun by the caterpillar. A cocoon is just a constructed silk casing used by moths and certain other types of insects. We have all read "the hungry caterpillar " book it states a cocoon not a chrysalis which is wrong but that caterpillar also eats ice cream and strawberry. It's not a guide book just a story.

Food and eggs

The main food for monarch caterpillars is the swan plant or milkweed (Asclepias fruiticosa). Plants can be grown from seed in late winter in a heated area, or purchased in early spring. Some garden centre swan plants may already have eggs on them, but if not, place the plants outside in a sunny spot so female monarchs can find and lay their eggs on the underside of a leaf. It is best to have only two or three caterpillars on each plant because they are very hungry creatures and will potentially eat a whole plant in days, especially in the last instar stages. If there are too many caterpillars on a plant, there will be insufficient amounts of food for them and they will be left starving and searching for food.

The monarch emerges

Diagram courtesy of www.learnaboutnature.com

This is perhaps the most exciting part of raising butterflies, but it happens very quickly and can easily be missed. Butterflies usually emerge mid morning if the surroundings are light and warm. When the butterfly emerges, the chrysalis splits at the bottom and the head pops out first. The monarch will usually cling to its empty chrysalis shell with its legs, as its wings will be very wrinkly and small at first sight. Then fluid from the abdomen pours into the wings to form large firm wings. It is very important not to disturb the monarch at this stage because any handling may permanently damage its wings, leaving it unable to fly. Every visible part of the caterpillar will be gone, in its place is a beautiful monarch butterfly. The new monarch will open and shut its wings, becoming stronger each time until it is ready to fly and start its journey as a butterfly.

Ready to fly

Monarchs that emerge in the morning can be released at the end of the day, or kept until the following day without needing to be fed. Those emerging in the afternoon should be released the next day. It is best if they are released on a warm sunny day, near flowers if possible for the best chance of survival. If it is colder than 16 degrees, they often cannot fly. Wait for the wings to dry before releasing the monarchs outside in the fresh air. Monarchs rely on the sun's heat rays for energy for flight. When the monarch is ready to make its first flight, place the butterfly on your finger and release it outside, perhaps making a wish in your head for the monarch to have a safe happy life. The monarch will then flutter into the skies above, flapping its wings faster and faster. The only goal in life for an adult monarch is to reproduce, although as a pollinator, they play an enormously important role in our planet's ecosystem. Most monarchs taste bad to birds and wasps and are generally left alone, due to all the cardenolides in their bodies (that they ingested as caterpillars via the nutrients in the swan plants).

How to differentiate between male and female monarchs

The male butterfly has two black spots either side of his wings, these are scent glands. Their black veins are also thinner than the female veins. The female has no dot markings on her wings and is slightly smaller than the male monarch.

Monarchs mating

I was lucky enough to witness this, when my son found these two monarchs in the driveway. He quickly picked them up to show me saying, "Look Mum, they are stuck together". The romance includes aerobatic flying and dancing together which can last up to six hours.

The five instar stages

The instar stages occur when the caterpillar outgrows it skin five times, in a manner similar to snakes. Each time it gets too big for its skin, it will move away to shed it, and then go back to its host plant to feed. You may see some black dead skin hanging on the swan plant when you next look. This means that a caterpillar has moulted (shed its skin). The intervals between moults are called instars and happen over a two week period.

Caterpillars 1st Instar
A newly hatched monarch larva is pale green or grey/white, shiny, and almost translucent. It has no stripes or other markings. The head looks black, with lighter spots around the antennae and below the mouthparts, and may be wider than the body. You will notice a small circular feeding pattern on the leaf, which is an easy way to indicate the egg has hatched and the tiny caterpillar is starting to eat. Time in this larval stage is usually one to three days. It's great to get children to use a magnifying glass at this stage to observe. Approximate length of body 2-6mm.

Caterpillars 2nd Instar
This larva has the distinctive yellow, black, and white stripes associated with monarchs. The front tentacles are easily visible, but the back tentacles are still barely visible. Monarchs are in the 2nd instar for one to three days. Approximate length of body 6-9mm.

Caterpillars 3rd Instar
The black and yellow stripes are more distinct than in younger caterpillars. The back tentacles (later to be antennae) are clearly visible and the front tentacles would extend to the tip of the head if they were bent forward. Monarchs are in the 3rd instar for one to three days. Approximate length of body 10-14mm.

Caterpillars 4th Instar
Fourth instar larvae have a distinct banding pattern on the thorax which is not present in third instars. The first pair of legs is even closer to the head, and there are white spots on the prolegs that are more conspicuous than in the third instar. Approximate length of body 13-25mm.

Caterpillars 5th Instar
The front tentacles of the 5th instar often extend past the head until they droop. Distinct white patches are found on the prolegs. They move much farther and faster than other instars, and are often found far from swan plants as they seek a site for pupating. Time in this stage is usually three to five days, temperature dependent, until they become a pupa (chrysalis). Approximate length of body 25-45mm.

This photo below was not staged I found them like this, as a happy family, theres even an egg!

Frequently asked questions

Can you feed your caterpillars pumpkin if you run out of swan plants?
Pumpkin is OK for emergencies but not recommended for the entire life cycle. Best given in the last instar stage, (ie at least ten days old or more than 4 cm in length). Any earlier than this and the caterpillars will not get enough cardenolides (nutrients) and will not be able to successfully transition to adulthood. Beware also that their frass (poop) turns orange!

How long do monarchs live for?
Average lifespan is six to eight weeks for summer generations and six to eight months for winter generations. Once the females and males have mated and the eggs have been laid, their job is done for the butterfly kingdom.

Where can I get swan plants in New Zealand?
Most garden centres sell swan plants in season (typically October - April). In peak summer months Mitre 10 Mega and other garden centres often sell out, so its best to ring first to see if there are any in stock and save yourself a journey.

How can I tell a male from a female monarch?
Males have a black spot on each of their hindwings, which are scent glands. They also have thinner veins (lines) on their wings than female monarchs. (see diagram on page 20).

My butterfly is stuck in its chrysalis, should I help it?
When monarchs get 'stuck' in their chrysalises, do not try to help them. It is a bad sign and is probably a case of the nasty OE spore. Euthanise the monarch as quickly as possible and be sure to sanitise EVERYTHING, including your hands to prevent spreading of OE disease.

Where do butterflies spend the night?
At night, or during stormy weather, most monarchs perch on the underside of a leaf, crawl deep between blades of grass, into a crevice in rocks, or holes in tree trunks, and sleep.

Why do new monarchs hang upside down when they have just emerged?
Butterflies hang upside-down when they emerge from their chrysalises so that gravity can help them pump the fluid from their abdomens into their wings. This allows the wings to expand and dry so that the monarch can use them to fly.

Are the spots around the top of the chrysalis real gold?
A group of researchers in Germany did a careful study of the properties of these spots. They are not metallic (so they aren't really gold), but the cells reflect light like metals do, giving them the appearance of being metallic.

Why do I have no eggs on my swan plants?
This is a common question that I receive a lot. Butterflies need nectar as a source of food, so you need to have nectar flowers in your garden as well as swan plants. I can assure you when it's warm enough and you have both swan plants and nectar flowers, the monarchs will lay eggs.

Can monarch butterflies survive in cold weather?
If temperatures are too cold, they can freeze to death. Wet, cold monarchs are in particular danger, ice can form on the butterfly which can kill. Monarchs can't fly unless they can warm their muscles to 13°C. If you see a monarch on the ground in winter, warm it up in your hands gently for a few minutes and then open up your hands. Hopefully the monarch is warm enough to fly away.

Do monarchs sleep?
Butterflies do not have eyelids, so they rest with their eyes open. At night butterflies find a sheltered spot and hide. They become quiescent. This quiescence, or resting, is not equivalent to human sleep.

How can we help boost the population of the monarch butterfly?

A good way to help is by planting swan plants early in greenhouses (or sunny rooms) in late winter or early spring. Ensure you cover the seedlings with a net as they grow to prevent the monarchs laying eggs too early. Seedlings never recover if eaten so early. If allowed to, these plants will get very bushy around January and be ready for the monarchs to lay their eggs on.

Why haven't I seen any monarchs this summer yet?

You don't see an abundance of monarchs until the summer weather really kicks in and it becomes settled and warm. Could you be living rurally near to fields where farmers are spraying pesticides on their crops? This can kill butterflies and other insects. Have you got enough or any nectar flowers as a food source for the butterflies in your garden?

It's winter and the weather conditions outside are freezing. Can I keep my monarchs inside?

Just be careful of any kitchen sprays or cleaning products that you have in your home, as these are harmful. Normally I keep my monarchs inside for a few days until I see a clear patch of warm sunshine in the forecast. I keep mine in my walk-in wardrobe where the monarch thinks it's winter as it's dark, and goes into diapause. If you keep them near light, they will think it's summer time and want to flutter around the house, stressing out flying into windows.

Why is it called a chrysalis and not a cocoon?

Monarch caterpillars form a chrysalis, which is the hard outer case enclosing the caterpillar where the transformation of turning into a beautiful butterfly begins. Moths form a silk which is spun and made out of silk. Many people question this, as they remember reading it in the popular book, "The very hungry caterpillar", which wrongly states that it's a cocoon.

What can I feed a monarch butterfly?

Nectar can be given by offering fresh flowers that are in your garden or a slice of orange or watermelon if you have some. Alternatively, you can easily supply a sugary solution to feed your butterfly too. You can dissolve sugar or honey in water, diluted as 7 parts water and 1 part sugar, and leave it in a small, shallow dish so the butterfly doesn't drown when feeding. Mix this solution well and refresh it every day.

What pests harm caterpillars and monarch butterflies in New Zealand?

Wasps are the most dangerous threat to caterpillars. Domestics cats are also known to kill monarch butterflies that have just eclosed out of their chrysalis. Ants, earwigs and snails love to snack on the eggs and spiders are known to eat tiny caterpillars.

How many kinds of butterflies are there in the world?

There are approximately 20,000 species of butterflies in the world.

What do the children learn?

Children feel great joy as well as gaining heaps of knowledge from learning about and observing the metamorphosis of the monarch butterfly. They learn to care for and show empathy towards the animal kingdom. They are drawn to the monarchs as they are a harmless yet beautiful creature, and caterpillars are not too creepy for them, or too tingly if placed on their hand. Having monarchs and caterpillars around is an excellent way of teaching young children about the insect life cycle, food requirements, pest control and overall awareness of the world around them. We need children to be taught about the importance of caring for the monarchs as they are an endangered species. Children will show incredible protectiveness towards these tiny living creatures as the caterpillars grow and change. Showing children how to grow swan plants and have a butterfly garden at home will hopefully give them knowledge to pass on to the next generation. Children like to care for animals and insects, but not all children have pets at home, so this gives them a sense of responsibility early in life. Children will soon become very involved and will check daily on their plants. Plus they will get so excited counting the number of caterpillars and chrysalises they have.

Monarchs offer a compelling introduction to insect life cycles, the details of eco systems and food webs, and the balance of nature. Plus it gets children into the great outdoors, discovering other plants and creatures. Having butterflies at home or around the classroom shows children that the odd caterpillar or chrysalis could die and they have to be careful of all insects as they can be delicate. It teaches responsibility. Living things die if they are mistreated or not taken care of properly, and entrusting a child to take care of the living parts of their environment means they'll learn what happens when they forget to water a plant, or pull a flower out by its roots. Through learning with the monarchs, children will also take an interest in other insects, and ask many questions. This is great as they are having to think and brainstorm about how the animal kingdom works and how humans have an effect on other animals and the environment around them. It teaches responsibility. A sense of belonging is evident when all the children gather together around the table, studying the caterpillars or chrysalises.

They will talk, and ask questions amongst themselves, learning together, and if they don't know an answer to their questions they can find books on insects and butterflies at their school or local library. Metamorphosis is also a great starting point for artwork to represent the learning on the monarchs and caterpillars and children will really get involved, expressing what they have seen and learnt in class. The children will then take the artwork home and share with family and friends and may also want to create a butterfly garden. In modern urban life, there's very little opportunity to interact so closely with nature. By bringing monarchs into the classroom you are incorporating science, high end thinkers, expression within their artwork, and maths.

(below photos of my children Lola, Lucas and Felix)

My daughter Lola has learnt so much about caring for caterpillars that she nearly knows as much as I do, and loves to finish my sentences when I'm teaching a class and I've brought her along. I sometimes get her to help and talk when I'm teaching in schools if she's available.

I have talked to a wide range of children from three to nine years of age over the last few years around New Zealand. I see joy in the children's eyes when I'm teaching them fascinating facts about the monarchs, and I know they truly care for their planet and the caterpillars. I see their curiosity and their gentleness when I give them magnifying glasses so that they can see the caterpillars up close. This is why I will continue teaching, although I can relax a little as there are so many amazing gifted teachers out there teaching the children about nature from an early age, with so much drive and passion. It makes me feel so blessed when they are surrounded by nature in their classrooms and in their outdoor areas. Some children I have visited twice and I'm astounded by how much they remember from my first talk, they soak in all the information because this is a subject they get excited about.

I witness a beautiful energy of enthusiasm from the children all wanting to ask questions when I enter their classrooms. Such excitement when I bring in live caterpillars on swan plants and nectar flowers. They rush to tell me how many swan plants they have at their homes or tell me the interesting places where they remember chrysalises hiding. I honestly love listening to their stories about raising caterpillars with their family. The follow-on effect is they will want to plant vegetables and flowers from seed, and help their parents in the garden, sharing the same interests and being part of it all.

Monarchs can also stimulate new forms of discovery within children and help them make connections to the natural world around them, getting the children out into their gardens with their own little area of swan plants and other flowers. They will interact meaningfully with their surroundings, plus think more freely. There have been many studies showing that being outside (within nature) is great for children's wellbeing. I believe monarchs are the doorway to a world of magic in nature and the world of butterflies, and a child's curiosity of other butterflies will soon start and they may become interested in red and yellow Admirals that are native to New Zealand. I have also found that many children soon click on to growing their own swan plant seeds and nurturing these seedlings, to sell these swan plants 3 or 4 months later as a fund raiser for their scout groups or schools. Excellent knowledge has been gained via the re-potting of seedlings, planning ahead for the summer season, and the ability to make easy money for a great cause. This is also a great way of raising awareness of the monarch butterflies to new people.

Overwintering in New Zealand

The overwintering stage in New Zealand starts in April or May. This is when swarms of monarch butterflies come together each year to overwinter at places around the country.

On warm sunny winter days (when temperatures are over 16 degrees), if you are lucky, you may see many monarchs gliding around looking for nectar nearby. Most of the time, however, monarchs will hang together from branches totally still and peacefully protecting each other. Monarchs are cold-blooded, they do not use much energy. In the cool temperatures, they burn their food reserves slowly. They eat very little during winter months.

When the monarchs form in big clusters they are known to be in "Diapause" (resting, hanging for the winter). Many of these butterflies survive the whole winter as a dormant group, only to revive and mate the following spring (around September or October) when the warmer weather sets in. The monarchs that overwinter in the trees live for about 7 to 9 months; that's if they survive the strong frosts, storms, hail and wind conditions through the harsh winters. This is different to the monarch butterflies that emerge during the summer months and who only live for approximately 6 to 8 weeks once they have mated and laid all their eggs.   Their job is done for the insect kingdom.

Temperature and food supply have a big influence on the size of the next summer's monarch population. A few cold, bitter winters and heavy rain may result in a drastic reduction in the number of monarchs and it will take a few years for numbers to re-establish again. In saying that, I've also witnessed hundreds of monarchs clinging in the trees without letting go while it's been blowing a gale! They seem such small and fragile creatures, yet they are resilient to the winds and strong enough to cling on to the branches with their feet as they swing side to side. This is why they choose to form clusters in trees that have shelter from the brunt of the winds – monarchs are so clever!

In Auckland it's quite common to get caterpillars all year round, although numbers are hugely reduced and far fewer sightings of monarchs occur in the winter. Whereas in the South Island we're only able to see monarchs in winter at the overwintering sites due to the difference in climate. Visiting these parks with your children and family is amazing, so take a picnic and your camera. Relax while enjoying the experience above you in the trees. Abberley and Woodham park in Christchurch are great for kids as the monarch butterflies are quite low down and my toddler even gets to spot them, before quickly returning to kicking and crunching the leaves on the ground.

The colours in the parks are so vibrant at this time of year; I'm beginning to enjoy autumn more and more each year. At first, you may not spot the clusters as sometimes a bunch of monarchs will look like a branch of dead leaves just hanging in the tree.

Be patient and have a good look around, also try to go on a sunny day and you'll see them gliding around you looking for nectar in the park. Luckily, the people of Christchurch are spoilt and have many places to spot the large clusters of monarch butterflies. I'm fortunate to have at least 6 overwintering parks within 10 minutes drive of my house to visit regularly.

Below I've put together an updated list for autumn 2019. I can confirm these are current overwintering spots in New Zealand. Please share the list which is available on my website and tell your friends, pre-schools, and family. By sharing and having easy access to this list which can be found on my website www.thebutterflymusketeers.com. We can all experience this magnificent joy, and witness nature at its best. It's absolutely amazing! The magical thing that I don't understand, which astounds me, is how these infant monarch butterflies know where to return for the winter, to a place their ancestors gathered the year before, without ever having been there before themselves. It is believed that monarchs leave behind a pheromone so that the next generation of butterflies can come back the following year to the same tree and form large clusters. A group of butterflies is called a kaleidoscope.

Spring is a critical time of year for the monarch butterflies, as this is when the numbers are at their lowest point of the year, the monarchs are weak and the old generation is dying. These monarchs are easy to identify, they look faded, tattered and may have parts of their wings bitten. They are also in need of nectar flowers, so make sure you have flowers blooming in spring ready for them to feast on. These monarch butterflies will lay eggs in the spring, so make sure you are growing heaps of swan plant seedlings at this time ready for summer. Or perhaps have a couple of plants ready for them to lay their first round on eggs on, and these new butterflies will become the first generation of the summer monarchs, that will last on average 4-6 weeks.

Christchurch
- Burnside Park
- St James' Park - Papanui
- Risingholme Park - Opawa
- Abberley Park - St Albans
- Pioneer Recreation Centre
- Redwood Park
- Woodham Park - Linwood
- Bishopdale Park
- North Canterbury – Victoria Park
- Larch Reserve – Casebrook
- Rawhiti Domain – North New Brighton
- Denton Park – Hornby
- Linwood Cemetery
- Edmonds Factory Garden - Woolston

Nelson
- Washbourn Gardens

South Canterbury
- Temuka Recreation Reserve – Temuka
- Aigantighe Art Gallery - Timaru
- Ashbury Park – Timaru
- Timaru Botanic Gardens
- Temuka golf course
- Oamaru Public Gardens

Palmerston North
- Apollo Park - Milson

Hamilton
- Hamilton Gardens Cobham Drive

Whakatane
- Warren Park

Auckland
- Jellicoe Park – Onehunga
- Blockhouse Bay Recreational Reserve

Threats to monarch butterflies

The removal of the monarch habitat happens when developers build large sub divisions destroying the natural landscape where swan plants once lived amongst the nectar flowers. Less plants means less butterflies, it's that simple. Humans are also a threat to monarchs and other pollinators when we use chemical sprays or weed killers.

Pesticide sprays on crops or gardens hang around in the air and linger on plants, eventually infecting and harming the monarchs. I learnt the hard way when I bought swan plants from a retailer that had been mistakenly sprayed with pesticides, only to discover a day later that approximately 70 of my caterpillars had been poisoned and died. In another instant I had heaps of caterpillars, that died within 24hrs due to my next door neighbour who booked in the spider proofing man round to her house!! Chemicals were sprayed a few metres from all of my swan plants in one of the windiest North West Canterbury spring days!! Luckily I witnessed the truck driving past my house, otherwise I would have been wondering what I did wrong and why they had become sick. It just goes to show that no matter how many plants you grow spray free from seed and take care of your caterpillars, outside influences can kill beyond our control.

Wasps are a problem especially if you live in Auckland, Nelson, Queenstown or Kaikoura. There are three main wasps in New Zealand: Paper wasps, Common wasps and the German wasps. They eat the monarchs' eggs, and caterpillars in various stages of their life cycle. Thankfully towards the end of the summer wasps actually change their dietary requirements from protein to nectar. If you have a lot of wasps around and you know where they are nesting, contact your local council who can get rid of a wasp's nest. If you still have the odd wasp, and you want to fully protect your caterpillars it's best to invest in a large caterpillar castle (zip mesh cover). You can then place your swan plants under this to protect them. This is also a good idea once you have enough eggs on your plants, as monarchs will not be able get inside to lay more eggs. Having a caterpillar castle is a great resource for your chrysalides too as they will hang at the top, and also caterpillars won't escape looking for sticks to hang on. As well as wasps, the caterpillars can also be attacked by the praying mantis so watch out for these creatures too in your garden.

Another major threat to the monarch is climate conditions such as bad winds, drought, unseasonal storms and rain. A harsh cold winter can also have a dramatic effect on the population of the monarchs as they are very sensitive to temperature change. Monarchs rely on the weather and environmental cues (temperature in particular) to trigger reproduction, migration, and hibernation. In the USA they have mosquito spraying trucks that drive around spraying harmful chemicals in the air. This can hurt butterflies if the truck gets close enough to the butterfly areas. I have read about many caterpillars getting sick because of this procedure. Although in the USA, mosquito spray is essential to prevent diseases spread by mosquitoes such as the Zika virus. Thankfully this doesn't happen here in New Zealand. However, living rurally near agricultural areas means there can be less wildlife due to the sprays farmers use on their crops.

Left below; "the awesome, healthy, summer foursome". Right below; toxic swan plants that had been unknowingly sprayed with pesticides.

How can we help save the monarch butterflies?

We can all do our bit individually, as every little gesture makes a difference.

- Avoid pesticides.
- Buy swan plants and plant them around your school, business and community areas in a sunny sheltered spot.
- Plant nectar flowers at home, schools, community areas and business gardens.
- Get involved in monarch habitat conservation in your local community parks.
- Spread the word and get school children and pre-schoolers involved from an early age having monarch butterflies around in classrooms and playgrounds.
- Educate people that the monarch butterfly is an endangered species and that we have to plant swan plants for monarchs to lay their eggs on so they can reproduce.
- Tag monarchs butterflies so we know more about there whereabouts.

Tagging monarchs begins in the autumn, as this is the generation of monarchs that go into the diapause stage. It is the monarch butterflies that hatch late in summer that we need more information on, as we don't know exactly where they go in the winter, or how far they fly. In spring do they go back to the same garden that they emerged from and used to fly in the previous summer?   It's free to tag monarchs, and for full information you can visit *www.monarch.org.nz* and request a pack of stickers. Then you can start tagging the monarchs. First you must enter the unique sticker number (stuck on your monarch) into the online database, stating when and where you released the butterfly. When someone else finds the monarch that you tagged, data is once again entered online, detailing where the monarch was spotted. You will get an automated update which is exciting, finding out where your monarch butterfly flew to.

Sustainability - Growing your own swan plants from seed

Swan plants can be grown easily from seed from August onwards, in a warm greenhouse or a kitchen window sill. Ensure that the seed bed does not dry out and is kept moist. There is a germination period of three weeks to a month, as the shell of the seed is hard. It's best to wait until there is good root formation before transplanting into the garden (see middle photo below). You need to let the plants grow about 30 cm high before taking them outside. I've seen four or five large caterpillars eat a big new plant in a couple of hours! Plants can get up to six feet (two metres tall) if allowed to. They usually do not bear seeds until the second year. In each seed pod (bottom left photo) is approximately 60 seeds. Ensure that you only water your plants in the morning or evening, as water evaporates in the mid day sun and burns the petals and leaves. You can also take cuttings from your healthy plants, by cutting the top of the swan plant off. Make sure you have counted four leaf nodes down from the top of plant, this is where you snip it (approximately 10cm long - see bottom right photo - cut where my thumb is). Make sure you cut the stem at an angle and place in a vase of water, after removing all the leaves bar the small top ones. The roots will slowly begin to grow and then you can place the seedling in the soil or a pot ready for the next season. Remember to wash your hands after. Growing from seed is a great way of saving yourself money and making sure you never run out of swan plants for your caterpillars when shops sell out during peak season. Plus you know they are spray free as your have grown them yourself.

North American migrating

Monarch butterflies have dazzled people around the planet for years. Every autumn, a spectacular natural phenomenon can be observed in the forested mountains, 10,000 feet high, 60 miles west of Mexico City. Hundreds of millions of monarchs migrate over 2000 kilometres from Canada and North America to eventually arrive in a remote area they have never been to before. To a place in the Mexican mountains that has its own microclimate with ideal temperature, humidity and elevation for the monarchs. Named Sierra Chincua, situated in the state of Michoacán. It is a mystery how the monarchs know how to fly there. Whether they follow the sun, or landscapes or even magnetic fields, this amazing process makes the monarch butterfly one of the most magnificent animals on the planet. This is remarkable for a creature with such fragile wings.

Changes in the temperature and length of daylight hours mean the monarch instinctively knows when summer is ending, and their bodies react accordingly, by delaying their reproductive maturity. This is the start of their incredible journey flying south for winter, roughly two months later they finally arrive at their overwintering sanctuary. If it's too cold the monarch cannot fly as their wings become sluggish, yet in the blazing hot sunshine they can over-heat. Most monarchs like to fly when it's warm, often stopping for nectar and water along the way. Each time they land there are enemies such as spiders or birds, along with potential poisonous pesticides that float around in the air. Some even have to fly across the Great Lakes which are situated in the Midwest region. Bad weather and unseasonal storms can be deadly when migrating south to Mexico. Soaring is the key to reaching their destination, this is when the monarchs fly with the thermal pressure rising from the ground heat of the sun, and they can glide and save energy by not flapping their wings. The monarch butterflies take advantage of ascending warm air currents and have a free ride. Amazingly these overwintering sites were not even discovered until 1975! This was only after a lengthy investigation involving a tagging program that saw thousands of monarchs fitted with tiny wing tags.

Map: Chris Brackley/Canadian Geographic. Range and migration information based on monarch butterfly fall and spring migrations map www.monarchwatch.org

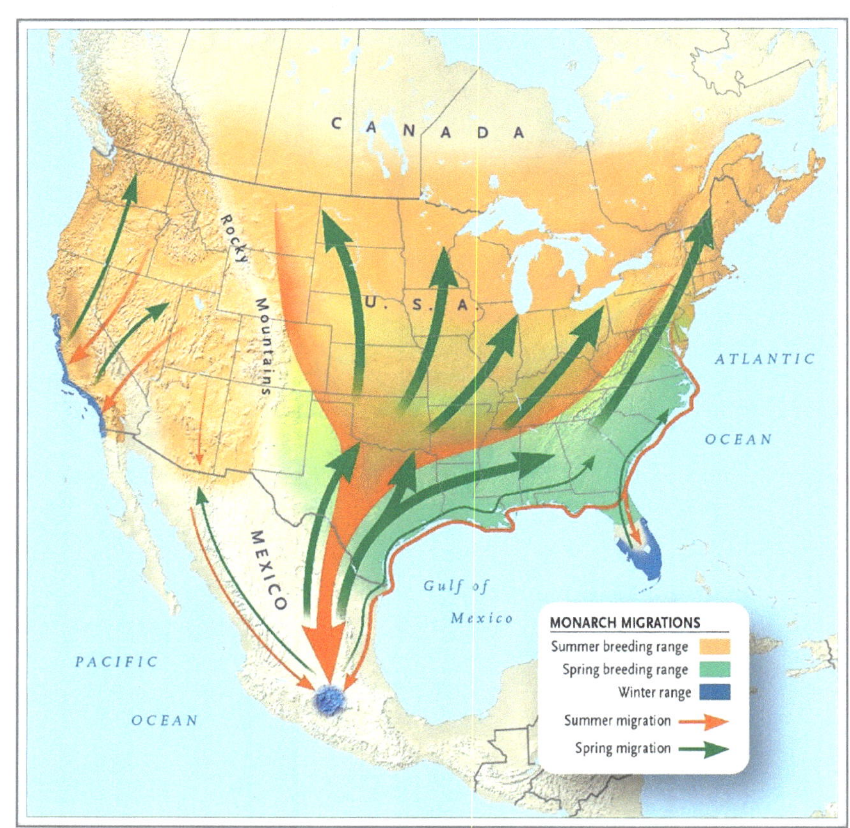

North American migrating

In Michoacán, Mexico, hundreds of hectares are being levelled by logging, and less trees mean the monarch butterflies are threatened, as they need the trees for warmth and protection from the cold and wind. The Mexican government has made logging near the sanctuaries illegal, but enforcement is difficult in such remote regions. By destroying this habitat and clearing the trees, the monarchs will have nowhere to hang over winter and may freeze to death. With the sanctuaries disappearing and bad weather, this is disastrous for the butterfly population. There has been a big focus in recent years on educating local residents about the harmful effects that logging can have in the area, and the importance of the natural wonder of the monarch butterfly overwintering sites. The logging has now been greatly reduced and effort is being made to turn Sierra Chincua into an attractive and eco-friendly tourist destination.

There are three theories that scientists think lead the butterfly to travel this incredible distance from Canada to Mexico, but it is currently an unsolved mystery.

- Specific cells in the butterfly brain regulating their internal clock and keeping them on course.
- Magnetic earth fields providing a subtle orientation guide.
- Navigation following a specific angle of the sun in relation to the earth.

The monarchs remain in their clusters all day and night during the winter months, resembling a bunch of dried leaves. After five months in the trees, spring arrives and the monarchs bloom again, slowly opening their wings to the sun, warming up for the flight back north. Physical activity increases within the monarch colony, as their sexual organs reach maturity and mating begins. Most of the monarchs will travel back to Texas eventually heading further north, pausing to mate, and producing new generations on the way. The second, third and fourth generation monarchs will arrive at the northern point from which previous generations departed (North America and Canada). It usually takes four generations to complete the round trip. Each monarch butterfly flies on its own, to a place it has never been.

The methuselah generation (sometimes called the super generation) are the generation of monarchs that emerge in late summer. They will live around nine months until spring when they are ready to mate. There is still much to be learned about monarch migration. For example, how do changing environmental conditions in late summer turn off reproduction in the emerging adults and "flip their switches" to start flying south? The real secrets of why and how monarchs migrate to the exact spots that they do, still remains trapped within their genes. *A staggering 99% of monarch eggs and caterpillars do not survive to become adult butterflies. That is why, for the remaining 1%, it is necessary to ensure that the monarchs are not threatened and survive so that the critical mass required to sustain their migrating and overwintering population is conserved and maintained. *

If you want to learn more about the migration from Canada/USA to Mexico I would throughly recommend watching a wonderful movie called *Flight of the Monarchs* which can be shown to children too (it's only 44 minutes long and available on Netflix). It is a scientific detective story about Dr. Fred Urquhart and his wife, Norah. They began the tagging project which eventually lead to the discovery of the monarch butterflies' secret hideaway in January 1975. Fred and Norah eventually set foot in the Mexican sanctuaries to witness with their own eyes the millions of monarchs in January 1976. They had uncovered the most incredible migration on earth. Thankfully in 2008, UNESCO declared the Monarch Butterfly Biosphere in Mexico a World Heritage Site.

*Source *Flight of the Monarchs*

Taking care of your chrysalides

Your chrysalis doesn't need food or water. If your swan plants are inside then an occasional misting of the swan plant will help keep the environment humid, which is necessary for a healthy chrysalis. Caterpillars will stop eating and start crawling away from their host plant trying to find the safest place to form a chrysalis, mainly hiding under other plants in the garden. They like part shade as the chrysalis sometimes burns and drys up in the sun's rays in peak summer. I still get blown away by the way gold dots appear around the top of a healthy chrysalis. I have found caterpillars half way down my driveway, many metres away from their original home, that I have had to rescue and put safely on a suitable plant before someone steps on them.

In summer, metamorphosis from caterpillar to monarch butterfly (ie the chrysalis stage), takes up to three weeks. Late forming monarch butterflies will stay in their chrysalis throughout winter but I have experienced monarchs emerging from this state after 10-12 weeks as healthy adult butterflies. Remember that your diapausing chrysalises are still alive. If the chrysalis has fallen off a stick, you can hang it by placing a dot of hot glue on a piece of paper and then placing the tip of the chrysalis in the slightly cooled (but still liquid) hot glue. Hold the chrysalis on the paper for a few seconds to allow the glue to harden. My preferred method is to tie some string around the cremaster (black hook) and then tape the string onto somewhere safe, like the edge of a shelf with plenty of room below so the monarch can hang their wet wings.

A chrysalis will become darker and then look transparent a couple of days before the monarch butterfly is ready to hatch. Keep a careful watch, as it only takes a few minute for a monarch to emerge from of its chrysalis! In some cases, it can take up to 45 minutes, but these monarchs are likely to have irregularities or diseases and will be weak. If the chrysalis has been very dark for at least five days and you cannot see the orange wings through the transparent casing, the monarch butterfly inside is probably dead and it will then dry up. The chrysalis below is hanging on a fuchsia flower camouflaged from predators. I captured this photo after the rain drops had fallen so eloquently onto it.

How to combat aphids

It is best to check on your plants daily to stay on top of the awful aphids that suck the life out of your swan plants, as well as stunting the growth and the ultimately destroying your plant. When plants are attacked by aphids, a sticky substance called honeydew is produced, accompanied by a black sooty coating on leaves turning the swan plant black. A couple of aphids on a plant one day, can turn into an army of aphids the next. The six different methods below should help, unless you want to be brutal and snip off the part of the plant that the aphids are on. Some people also recommend ladybirds, but they too may be predators as they can eat the monarch eggs.

RUB THEM OUT: This is what I find most effective, simply get rid of aphids by rubbing them off with your fingers and thumbs. This is effective when the numbers are low and if you're not afraid to get your hands dirty, this method you need to stay on top off and check daily for new aphids.

COMPANION PLANTING: Planting the following around your swan plants will hopefully keep your aphids at bay and reduce their number. Plants include chives, coriander, garlic, parsley, poppies, marigolds and nasturtiums. Luckily for me, my nasturtiums self seed from the previous year, which makes my job easier.

BRUSH THEM ASIDE: Use a clean paint brush to brush aphids off the swan plants and get in those nooks and crannies without damaging the plants. Keep your plants in a few places around your butterfly garden, which will stop the infestation spreading fast.

ESSENTIAL OILS: Create a mixture of equal parts thyme, peppermint, clove, and rosemary oils (4-5 drops of each should be enough). Mix this solution into a small spray bottle filled with water. Shake well and apply to infested plants. This potent mix of essential oils will kill most garden insect pests, but I would not recommend using this mix once you have eggs and caterpillars on your plants.

BLAST WITH A HOSE: Gently hold the swan plant with one hand to avoid breaking the stems whilst hosing the aphids off with medium amount of water pressure. Place the plant on its side away from other plants so you don't hose the aphids onto nearby plants.

HOT SOAPY WATER: Add a bit of washing up liquid into a spray bottle and shake, then rub all the leaves making sure the aphids are off. Make sure there are no eggs or caterpillars on the plants, then rinse your swan plant thoroughly with a hose.

The Butterfly Musketeers

The Butterfly Musketeers organisation was founded in 2013 by Maria Romero, a passionate butterfly rescuer and keeper of monarch butterfly gardens. My mission is to raise an awareness of these beautiful creatures and share with people how much can be learnt from the transformation from caterpillar to monarch by studying and caring for them.   The Butterfly Musketeers is a not for profit organisation who visits schools and shares knowledge, resources and passion to answer children's questions about the monarch butterflies. I can be booked via my website www.thebutterflymusketeers.com for school visits. There you will find more in-depth details about what I bring to the classroom and about my fun interactive talks. Talks run during terms 4 and 1 only of the school calendar (spring and summer).

The Butterfly Musketeers also help set up community events and give talks on monarchs butterflies. Host butterfly days at garden centres and garden clubs during the summer months too. We also visit local retirement homes, and will continue to do this, as there is such delight when the residents get a surprise visitor dressed up in monarch colours carrying a basket of newly emerged butterflies to be released in their communal gardens for all to see and enjoy. Each year the butterfly musketeers donates a large mural of a butterfly on a classroom wall, to a school that has gone beyond. By helping save the monarchs, raising caterpillars, growing heaps of swan plants and that the monarch butterfly life cycle has been a huge learning topic for them.

One of our goals is to plant in our gardens nectar flowering plants to feed the butterflies, as well as swan plants to attract monarchs to lay their eggs on. Over many summers we have seen so many injured and deformed monarchs arriving into our gardens, some just old and tired, or some just wanting to spend their last few hours with us. We give them love, some fruit and sugary water to enjoy and a safe place to rest away from predators. Wasps have been a big problem over the years around New Zealand, and witnessing a caterpillar being stung is awfully distressing. I have seen wasps sucking at the chrysalis until it's dead. To me this shows that we cannot save every monarch and at the end of the day they are part of the food chain, providing sustenance for those insects and birds higher up the food chain. Although sad at times, we have learnt that we must not get too attached to our monarchs. A female butterfly can lay up to 400 eggs in her life so even if two eggs develop into healthy monarchs then that's still progress. The Butterfly Musketeers help monarchs with broken wings and repair them in our homes so they are able to fly once again.

Therefore, instead of taking care of sick monarchs, you should put your energies into growing more swan plants for the monarchs to lay their eggs on and nectar flowering plants for the butterflies to feed on.   We have to be more sustainable, growing swan plants from seeds with love and nurture. Educate children on the process of metamorphosis, so the next generation will then have a more caring approach and kindness towards the animal kingdom. We need to help the monarchs for future generations to see the wonders nature has offered us so close up.

On my Facebook page, "The Butterfly Musketeers" we try to educate and inspire children and adults to care for these endangered species. It's a great page for butterfly lovers and enthusiasts. The page has helpful ideas and advice showing how to grow great butterfly gardens, plant nectar flowers, and attract and feed the butterflies. Plus we have updated information, videos, facts and photos. Nature is there to be enjoyed, to get outside and relax by watching the amazing phenomena of the metamorphosis cycle from the egg to the adult butterfly. People can share their photos, ideas, information, and successes with other passionate people. We can also inform you of current stock levels of swan plants in your community for the times when hungry caterpillars have stripped your plants bare. My Facebook page has been a powerful tool for parents to educate their children in understanding the monarchs, as well as opening up the new generation's passion and love for the monarchs. We are able to support a flourishing monarch population here in New Zealand, and also globally through social media. By learning about the monarch butterflies, people will often become interested in bees and other wonderful animals and insects that visit us in our homes and local environment. Our website has photos, stories about our school visits and current blogs. It's a knock-on effect, or in my case I would say 'The Butterfly Effect'!

Going forward I plan to work with some Christchurch schools to create bee and butterfly friendly gardens within their schools. We will do this with children of all ages, teaching them in small groups. By showing children how to sow their own seeds in their classrooms and once big enough, how to plant into their gardens, this will become a personal project. My fellow butterfly musketeers can gather their own research and study whilst gaining valuable knowledge along the way. They will be given a certificate for their care and hard work at the end of the project once all the nectar flowers and swan plants have been planted and the bees and monarchs have arrived.

I'm also truly ecstatic about collaborating with the "Guardians of Rawhiti Domain New Brighton" in Christchurch, a group of amazing people dedicated to giving back to the environment and children of the Eastern Suburbs. They are making Rawhiti Domain a flagship park, once again beautiful to attract bees, monarchs, native birds and plant species to an area that had been ruined in the earthquake. It's going to be a very special place to visit in times to come.

We also tag monarchs here in New Zealand in the autumn, so we can find out more about where they go over winter, and how long they live. This information is entered on a main database. Several hours after they have emerged and their wings have dried out, you can tag your monarch. It takes less than 30 seconds to tag a monarch, and tagging doesn't hurt the monarch. The sticker should be stuck on the hindwing (back wing) underneath side. Remember to make a wish when you have set a monarch butterfly free!

I have discovered that many teachers I meet buy endless amounts of swan plants each summer out of their own pockets for the enjoyment and education of their students. To help them build a swan plant collection for their schools, and help boost the monarch population, each Spring I organise #ProjectSwanPlant with over 130 schools. By collecting their own seeds at the end of the season, teachers will have a ready supply of swan plants for the caterpillars the following year. Growing seeds is so much cheaper, especially from seed pods. Many schools now are sowing seeds in bulk, so that once the seedlings are big enough they can sell as a fundraiser for their schools.

#ProjectSwanPlant has helped to counter the reduction of butterflies within the Eastern Suburbs where over 6000 homes and gardens were destroyed by the earthquakes. Those former gardens were an ideal food source for local butterflies and bees. Monarchs are great indicators of environmental change, as they are sensitive and have a recognisable appearance. Many butterfly species in large numbers indicate a healthy environment, whereas a lack of butterflies may indicate a change in the local environment.

The photo on the left is a tagged monarch.

My observations of Autumn monarchs

January to April 2019 proved to be an extremely long summer for Christchurch that didn't seem to want to end. Winter finally came for a few days here and there, with just a couple of frosts in May and June and no real chill factor until mid July.

What I observed that winter was that the caterpillars took a couple of days to turn into a chrysalis, instead of approximately one hour to form like they do in summer months. Monarchs are then likely to emerge deformed as most of their energy has been used up with the intense labour of forming into a chrysalis. Caterpillars also slowed down feeding on the swan plants as they were conserving their energy to keep warm. What I also found this year was the late season monarchs that emerged were sometimes smaller, as they hadn't eaten through as many swan plant leaves whilst caterpillars.

I noticed there is far higher risk to the monarch butterflies of OE and NPV disease if born in the autumn or winter months (further details on page 33). Most of the monarchs I watched emerging really struggled and hadn't got the energy or strength to hang onto their chrysalises to dry their wings once they emerged. I've been lucky to walk past and help a few and they have turned out beautiful as I hung them just in time, I just let them hang on my finger and carefully place them on a stick, stem or petal. The majority of my pupae stayed in chrysalis form for about six weeks or more instead of the normal two weeks in the summer.

Towards the end of May, I collected about 25 chrysalises that had hung themselves around my glasshouse. This was delicate work, carefully removing them by their hanging silk thread, then hot gluing this same thread onto a cotton bud, which I then put into a foam oasis (the hard sponge florists use to hold floral arrangements in place). This oasis I kept indoors, as if they were not freezing, the pupae had some chance of survival. I could also keep an eye on them more closely. About a third of these rescued chrysalises managed to pupate and emerge as adult butterflies, but most of them were noticeably smaller than normal. The ones that weren't able to fly, I fed a diet of mandarins, watermelon and sugary water. My monarch butterfly pets lived with me an average of six to eight days, although I've heard of monarchs lasting for a couple of months inside. Monarch butterflies don't need to eat as much in the winter, as when it is too cold they move into the diapause stage and basically hibernate. Below is a male monarch that was my last for the 2016 season. He was in his chrysalis for at least 12 weeks which is an extremely long time. He liked to hang on the trampoline on warm days but never got the hang of flying as he wasn't strong enough. He lived for about two weeks.

In the photo below, you can see the wing is not fully formed due to OE disease.

My observations of Autumn monarchs

This is no ordinary monarch butterfly in the photos below. I named her Lioness as she was full of strength and courage. This is one monarch I wasn't expecting at all. I had read about chrysalises not emerging all winter and waiting till spring to emerge, and I wanted to see for myself if this was true. Lioness was in her chrysalis for eight or nine weeks at least. As an experiment I left three chrysalises in my glass house to see if they could survive the harsh winter conditions. They were hanging on my geranium plants and on the side of pots. I checked on them once a week and thought, "no chance" but still I had a sneaky feeling and wanted to see what would happen. Some mornings the chrysalises were rock hard, and covered in ice, yet by the afternoon you could see the ice melting and dripping off. I wish I had taken photos as they looked so amazing.

Towards the end of the winter, I saw the chrysalises darkening and realised they weren't dead as I started to see the monarch wings. Such a surprise as I had totally forgotten about checking on them when it was so cold, and the last place I was going to hang out in was my greenhouse! One day I braved the freeze and decided to go into my glass house with a bleach solution (5% bleach 95% water) so I could wipe and wash all the many swan plants that were being protected from the ice and frosts, to eradicate disease and pests ready for the new season. Out of the corner of my eye I saw a monarch on the floor, I couldn't believe it. I was so happy that she had made it! Sadly the other two chrysalis didn't survive. Her proboscis was a little stuck, so I uncurled it with a pin and she could drink and eat, straight afterwards she would flap her wings. Lioness loved being on my hand and had some busy days doing somersaults on my flowers and jumping off and landing on the carpet. She seemed healthy apart from one twisted hindwing which she didn't like to show when her photo was being taken. The only monarchs I keep in my house are those that are unable to fly or have been hurt or rescued. I feed them daily with fresh cut flowers or just let them hang on the petals.

Monarch butterflies will not necessarily need feeding for the first 24 hours, and will feed less in winter months as they are mostly inactive. Although it's nice to have sugary water handy just in case they are thirsty. If the monarch butterfly does not unwind its proboscis after several tries, place a pin in the loop of the proboscis and pull the pin gently away from the head so the proboscis is extended and touches the sugary water. Once the proboscis is in the sugary water, the monarch will feed and you will see the proboscis moving forward and backwards inside the liquid. If you have swan plants and late season caterpillars during the winter months, it's not cruel to keep a monarch inside, safe from frosts and storms. I keep them on a plant in a dark corner of my house so they still know it's winter and they will go into diapause. I only release on warm sunny winter days, after feeding.

Above photos of my "Lioness" butterfly

Diseases that can occur when breeding monarchs

Bacterial and viral deaths are quite common in this particular species so if you have caterpillars that suddenly go limp or begin to ooze then it is possible that they've contracted a disease. If you have a chrysalis that suddenly goes brown or black, this could also mean it has contracted a bacterial infection. There are two diseases that harm the monarchs, OE (*Ophryocystis Elektroscirrha*) and NPV (*Nuclear Polyhedrosis Virus* or Black Death).

OE (Ophryocystis Elektroscirrha)

OE is a protozoan parasite that infects monarch butterflies. Protozoans are single celled organisms. The dormant cells live as spores on an infected monarch's abdomen, so that when she lays her eggs on the swan plant, both the egg and plant may become infected.

When the caterpillar hatches, it usually eats both egg casing and plant, thus ingesting the spores. Digestive chemicals cause the spores to break open and release the parasites. The damage is not visible on the caterpillar, but towards the end of the chrysalis stage, spotting (little black dots) can be seen through the cuticle wall. The butterfly will still try to emerge, but some maybe too weak even to escape the pupal casing, whilst others will not have the strength to fully expand and dry their wings and so will fall to the ground where they have little or no chance of survival.

Often times, the monarch caterpillar or chrysalis will die for no apparent reason. This does not mean that a protozoan has killed them, other causes of death could include ingestion of chemical toxins, a wound that became infected by opportunistic bacteria, or thermal stress caused by conditions that are too hot or too cold. Even a chemical spray from the kitchen or pesticides sprayed outside in the fields could adversely affect your monarchs. I mainly experience diseased monarchs at the end of the summer season, this is generally the case with most breeders, as diseases have had time to spread.

How to tell if butterflies are infected with OE

Do you see any unusual dirt-like spots on the caterpillar? The caterpillar may stop eating and hang from the swan plant by their prolegs, with the anterior and posterior ends drooping downwards. If so, chances are likely that your caterpillars have ingested the OE spore. If you suspect your butterfly has OE, releasing it will only spread the parasite to future monarchs. These butterflies are no good for the monarch kingdom and should be euthanised.

Keeping your caterpillars healthy

- Rinse off your swan plants before serving them to your caterpillars.
- Don't let butterflies emerge from their chrysalises above feeding caterpillars.
- Regularly clean out poop and caterpillar corpses.
- Disinfect your swan plants at the end of each batch, wiping the leaves down with a bleach solution (95% water and 5% bleach). This helps to get rid of spores.
- Rather than having the disease wipe out every plant and caterpillar, keep your swan plants in several different areas of your garden, which will help containment if you suspect disease.

NPV (The Nuclear Polyhedrosis Virus)

Caterpillars have no immune system so they cannot fight this disease. Whilst this is extremely rare in New Zealand, a sign of NPV is when your caterpillar looks oily and slick before they die. This process of slowly killing the caterpillar takes close to three days, the caterpillar eventually dies and turns to pure liquid. Any infected caterpillars should be removed and destroyed immediately upon awareness of the infection.

If disease or deformity is found, the quickest and most humane way you can euthanise a monarch is by wrapping it in a tissue and putting it in the freezer. This is a quick and painless method that many people use. Remember to dispose of the tissue and contents afterwards. It is not nice to witness a monarch butterfly struggling to fly and dying slowly as it cannot feed itself due to deformities and it's the kindest thing to do.

To keep disease at bay, remember to keep your plants and the areas where you have your swan plants clean and remove frass regularly. If you suspect you have a sick caterpillar, and see signs of green liquid on the caterpillar or plant, remove and isolate that caterpillar onto another plant, whilst keeping an eye on it in case its condition worsens. Also be aware when purchasing your plants as some may have been accidentally sprayed, which kills caterpillars within 24hrs or makes them sick.   When your are raising butterflies in large numbers you always have to show caution and put the time and effort in. If you are new to raising monarchs I suggest keeping your caterpillar numbers to a manageable amount of about 20 at a time.

Below pictures are monarchs with suspected OE that had struggled out of their chrysalises. They have crinkled twisted wings and are not completely formed. The monarch butterfly (bottom right) was flightless.

NPV chrysalises will go black and dull green and you cannot see the monarch inside
(bottom left).

Butterfly life cycle word search

```
N   E   C   T   A   R   T   N   M   M   E   G   G   K
D   W   T   Y   U   K   O   H   J   N   B   I   O   L
P   S   A   N   L   C   H   R   Y   S   A   L   I   S
U   A   S   Q   L   O   B   N   V   C   X   X   Z   A
P   S   D   W   M   I   G   R   A   T   I   N   G   Y
A   E   C   F   A   G   Y   U   I   O   O   P   H   M
U   E   A   T   L   N   S   S   A   A   F   L   O   E
L   M   T   R   L   S   P   D   A   S   C   I   J   T
O   E   E   E   I   Q   F   L   S   F   D   U   M   A
G   R   R   G   F   A   V   A   A   C   E   Y   H   M
D   G   P   K   E   D   B   R   S   N   A   Y   T   O
E   I   I   I   C   X   N   V   R   E   T   G   R   R
W   N   L   Y   Y   W   M   A   F   S   I   F   E   P
G   G   L   R   C   T   K   E   F   A   N   D   N   H
F   S   A   C   L   Y   O   P   C   F   G   S   Y   O
L   S   R   F   E   H   J   K   K   P   L   O   M   S
O   W   T   G   J   U   I   W   I   N   G   S   B   I
W   L   O   P   G   C   C   E   X   X   W   D   G   S
E   E   B   M   O   N   A   R   C   H   A   G   H   J
R   W   L   K   Q   R   R   H   Y   A   D   F   G   H
S   Y   U   J   G   B   U   T   T   E   R   F   L   Y
B   S   Z   A   S   T   O   P   C   K   A   S   W   T
```

EMERGING
LARVAE
EGG
CHRYSALIS
CATERPILLAR
METAMORPHOSIS
NECTAR
WINGS

BUTTERFLY
SWAN PLANT
EATING
MONARCH
PUPA
MIGRATING
FLOWERS
LIFE CYCLE

Discussion questions for the classroom

Did you know   ....

1. Did you know that caterpillars hatch from eggs? What other animals do you know hatch from eggs?

2. Did you know that a caterpillar gets a new skin coat when it outgrows its old skin? What other animals do you know that get a new skin?

3. Did you know butterflies have wings covered in tiny little scales that look like dust on your fingers when you hold the butterfly? What other animals do you know that have wings? How are butterfly wings different from bird wings? Does a butterfly have feathers?

4. Did you know that a butterfly is an insect? What other animals do you know that are insects?

5. Did you know that monarch butterflies are great travellers? Sometimes they fly for thousands of kilometres when the cold weather arrives, to places where it's much warmer for them. What other animals do you know that fly far away from the winter cold?

6. Do you know where the monarch butterfly got its name from? Early settlers who came to North America from Europe were impressed by the sight of the orange and black butterfly. So they named it "Monarch," after King William, Prince of Orange, state holder of Holland, and later named King of England. Do you know where your surname originated from?

18 Fun Facts

1. The female monarch can smell a swan plant from 2 kms away.

2. Monarch caterpillars become toxic to birds by feeding on swan plants.

3. Monarchs flap their wings between five and 12 times a second, which is about 300 to 720 times a minute.

4. Butterflies attach their eggs to leaves with a special glue.

5. When the caterpillar first emerges out of the egg, it will eat the egg first as it's full of protein.

6. Adult monarchs can fly between 80 - 130 kms in one day.

7. Caterpillar poop is called frass.

8. Monarch butterflies taste with their feet.

9. Monarchs may live from two days to approximately 9 months.

10. When the monarch butterfly caterpillar is two weeks old, it weighs 3,000 times as much as it did when it was born.

11. The monarch butterfly has three pairs of legs, giving it a total of six legs.

12. The common milkweed plant is called a swan plant for a reason! The flower pods that contain the seeds look like actual swans. These will appear at the end of the season if the hungry caterpillars don't strip the plant to just the stems, (which happens in the majority of cases). See photo below.

13. Monarchs undergo the longest recorded two-way migration of any insect. Up to four generations of monarch butterfly complete a round trip of approximately 8,000km.

14. A group of butterflies is officially called a kaleidoscope. They may also be called a swarm or flutter.

15. Monarch caterpillars have 12 eyes (six either side of their head).

16. Female monarchs normally start mating after 3 days of eclosing.

17. You can tell the gender of the butterfly while in chrysalis. A vertical line at the top of the first ring of chrysalis just below the two black dots means a girl. No line means a boy.

18 Monarchs don't eat for 24 hours after eclosing.

Butterfly poems

Caterpillars

What do caterpillars do?
Nothing much but chew and chew.

What do caterpillars know?
Nothing much but how to grow.

They just eat what by and by
will make them be a butterfly

But that is more than I can do
however much I chew and chew.

By Aileen Fisher

Butterfly Cycle

(to the tune of "Row, Row, Row Your Boat")

Hatch, hatch little egg,
I'm so very small.
Teeny tiny caterpillar,
You can't see me at all.

Crawl, caterpillar, crawl,
Munching on a leaf.
Crawling, munching, crawling, munching,
Eat and eat and eat.

Form, form chrysalis,
I'm a different shape;
Hanging by a silken thread
Until I can escape.

Rest, rest, chrysalis
While I change inside;
Now at last my time has come
To be a butterfly.

Stretch, stretch, pretty wings
It's a special day;
Soon they will be strong enough
For me to fly away.

Fly, fly, butterfly,
Fly from flower to tree;
Find a place to lay my eggs
So they can grow like me.

By Suzy Gazlay

The Fuzzy Caterpillar

(to the tune of "the incy wincy spider")

The fuzzy caterpillar
Curled upon a leaf,
Spun her little chrysalis
And then fell asleep.
While she was sleeping,
She dreamed that she could fly,
And later when she woke up
She was a butterfly!

Anon

Mr Monarch

A beautiful butterfly passes me by.
I see its bright colours flashing out of the sky.

Dancing through the trees, your wings are on fire. I try to touch you, but you just fly higher.

Please Mr monarch, come down and play. I reach out to you, but you fly, fly away.

By Christine Summers

Fuzzy Wuzzy

Fuzzy, wuzzy, creepy crawly
Caterpillar funny
You will be a butterfly
When the days are sunny.

Wiggling, flinging, dancing, springing
Butterfly so yellow,
You were once a caterpillar,
Wriggly, wiggly fellow.

By Lillian Vabada

Science questions on monarchs

1. Write four words that describe a monarch butterfly:

2. List the four stages of the monarch butterfly life cycle:

3. How many days approximately is it before the egg hatches into a caterpillar?

4. Count how many eggs, caterpillars and chrysalises you have in total?

5. If a chrysalis darkens what might it indicate?

6. Approximately how many eggs does a female monarch lay in her lifetime?

7. What can we do to help save the monarch butterflies?

8. What is the most amazing thing you have learnt whilst studying the life cycle of a monarch butterfly?

9. Why do you think there are less monarchs in New Zealand than there were 30 years ago?

Monarchs in the classroom; Activities

1. Design and make a monarch finger puppet or a caterpillar glove puppet.

2. Draw a giant caterpillar number chart, on each part of the body write the numbers 1 - 20.

3. Draw or print off a colour picture of a monarch and label parts of the monarch's anatomy. Then get the children to discuss the functions of the different parts.

4. Have a science table in the classroom with a couple of swan plants in pots. Make sure this area is kept clean of frass/poop each day. Also make sure there are not too many caterpillars on each plant as there needs to be enough leaves to go around.   Place a few small magnifying glasses next to the swan plant so children can observe the caterpillar from a very small size. Place a clipboard with paper so the children can record when the egg hatches, turns into a chrysalis and ultimately becomes a monarch. I've found mesh washing baskets from the $2 shop very useful when breeding monarchs.

I turned the washing basket upside down over the swan plant, which helps protect against little wandering hands. Also, if a monarch emerges over the weekend when the classroom is shut, it's contained and safe. Whereas a child might not see it if it's sitting on the floor when they next walk into class and tread on it.

5. Get the children to journal in a writing book their findings and what has happened or is happening with the caterpillars on the swan plants. Try to encourage the children to use scientific and descriptive words.

6. Investigate symmetry through art. Draw a butterfly and fold it in half so both sides are equal. Ask the children to match the shapes on both sides of the paper wings by drawing, cutting and sticking designs onto their cut outs.

7. Drip paint butterflies - draw a large butterfly with a vivid pen and cut out and drip paint on to the butterfly.

- Draw a butterfly on manila paper, then fold in half to make the shape of a large butterfly.
- Drip or brush paint along the middle of the fold to make the body of the butterfly.
- Drip pretty colours all over your paper.
- Fold the paper again and rub it with your hand.
- Open it out again and your butterfly will have lovely wing designs.
- Cut out your butterfly and paste it onto black card to place on the classroom wall.

8. Read the following story books about monarch butterflies to the class.

The Classroom Butterfly - by Dawn McMillan (Thomson Learning)
Katie's Butterfly by Jenny Giles (Thomson Learning)
Butterfly Day by Judy Raymond (Ready to Read)
Butterflies by Jo Windsor (Heinemann)
Making a Caterpillar (Thomson Nelson)
The Very Hungry Caterpillar by Eric Carle (Penguin Putnam)

9. How many small words can you find in the word CATERPILLAR?

Monarchs in the classroom; Activities Cont:

10. Print off and colour in the monarch on page 43.

11. Paint monarchs on glass windows, using a stained glass window effect.

12. Find big rocks and paint monarchs, caterpillars or flowers on them.

13. Plan a class outing to one of the many overwintering spots in local parks during the autumn months. This allows the children to witness a special event, which will raise many questions about the monarchs. Plus they will understand the final stage of the process and see where their monarchs have gone for the winter. Refer back to overwintering in New Zealand to find your local park. Make sure you visit the park beforehand to be certain the monarchs are there, as some years are better than others.

14. Make a butterfly mask - draw a butterfly and make two holes at the top for the eyes. Put another two smaller holes on the side and put string around the back. Use pipe cleaners for the antennae.

15. Draw the life cycle using a paper plate or piece of card. Let the children draw on paper first what they think is the right order. Divide the circle into 4 quarters with a black pen. There are many examples of this on Pinterest or Google images if you search for "monarch plate life cycle"

Materials suggested:
● Pasta - bowtie pasta for the butterfly and shell type pasta for the chrysalis
● White beans or balls (from inside a bean bag) for the eggs
● Paper plate
● Twigs and leaves
● Coloured pens
● Glue
● Labels - Eggs, Caterpillar, Chrysalis, Butterfly

16. Visit Butterfly Creek if you're near Auckland, The Butterfly and Orchid Garden in Thames, West Lynn Garden in Auckland or Otago Museum in Dunedin. All have butterfly areas and are great for school day trips.

17. Symmetry activity - print off pictures from the internet of insects that are half drawn and get the children to draw in the other side of the line to complete the whole insect.

18. Draw and label the parts of a butterfly. Ask the children to discuss the functions of the different parts.

19. Discuss and compare the differences between butterflies and frogs. Review all stages of the life cycles of a frog, where the frog lives, (water and land) what they eat, and about the transformation they go through.

20. Lastly my favourite! Make a mural on a classroom wall or playground fence. This will look totally awesome for everyone to see and stay around for years which will be so colourful. Children may draw caterpillars and butterflies, as well as other plants and animals. Draw your design on a large piece of paper first before copying on the wall.

Imperfections

This beautiful old butterfly arrived in my garden early March 2018. She spent at least 45 minutes in my garden before she eventually flew away.

I watched her sucking deep down with her proboscis into the nectar in my zinnia flower. She loved it and couldn't get enough, she was not scared of me even though I was up close watching her, and admiring her battered body. She must have had many stories to tell, and I wondered how far she had come from, I had many questions I'd have liked her to answer. I will never know I can only imagine. After having a big feed on my nectar flowers she then went on to lay at least 10 eggs on my swan plants. Monarch butterflies are here to show us how to never give up and grow old gracefully. She looked weathered and dull looking due to the intense sun, wind and rain.

Although her wings were damaged, she still got to where she wanted to go. It didn't stop her, I was surprised how she still showed immense strength and determination. She showed me patience, by taking her time to suck in the nectar and glide around in the air above me circling before coming back to the swan plant.

It's like that old saying "never judge a book by it's cover"; instead you should take the time to get to see into that person's or animal's soul or find out that stranger's story as we have all got a story to tell. You just got to give your time and be present with that person or within nature and your find out so much! This female monarch was different which is why I watched her, and shows us that it's good to be unique individuals because that's what makes our world so interesting. It would be very boring if we were all the same.

Sometimes we humans are quick to judge people by their looks and never see their inner beauty. At first I thought she was a damaged monarch that was on her last legs that couldn't fly as I've never seen such damaged wings in so many places before. I was happy to see that she still attracted male company and a male was flying around her. Again monarch teaches us that no matter how old or how we look we can always attract new friends and partners into our life. In the monarch's mind she was busy and she knew she had chores to do that day, have a big feed, fly around gracefully and lay eggs for the next generation of monarch butterflies that will overwinter around the Christchurch parks.Over the years monarchs always impressed me with how they fly around with damaged wings, or other times new born monarchs have refused to fly away off my hand as they knew there were days of torrential rain ahead and wanted to stay inside on my flowers. I am very thankful to this monarch butterfly for coming to my garden one hot Saturday afternoon while the kids were playing in the other garden and I got to spend time peacefully alone with her and watch her do acrobatics on my swan plants.

HOW TO SOW SWAN PLANTS FROM SEED

One of the best ways to make sure you have enough swan plants on hand to feed all those hungry munching Monarch caterpillars is to do a little planning ahead, and grow your own seeds. Plus, swan plant seedlings can be hard to find later in the growing season, particularly if the Monarchs have a bumper year and eat up large!

THE TEAM AT YATES HAVE PULLED TOGETHER SOME TOP TIPS ON PLANTING SWAN SEEDS:

1. You can sow **Yates Swan Plant Seeds** directly where they are to grow during Spring through to Autumn in the North Island, or from late Spring to early Autumn in the South Island (and colder areas of the North).

2. Or sow seeds earlier in the season in a glasshouse, or indoors on a warn windowsill, into seedling trays, or any container with some holes for drainage

3. Use a good quality seed raising mix that is fine and free draining

4. Scatter seed thinly, cover with seed raising mix (you are aiming for the seeds to be around 5mm deep), firm down and water gently

5. Seeds will germinate in 14-21 days

6. When you take them outside and transplant into the garden, we recommend soaking the seedling in **Yates Thrive Natural Seaweed** tonic (diluted 1-2 caps per bucket). This helps the roots re-establish quickly and prevents transplant shock, plus helps with improving plant resistance for protection against pests, drought and frosts.

7. Space your plants around 1m apart in the garden

8. Plants will grow to around 1.5m in height

9. Plants will flower in 14-16 weeks (if they get a chance – many swan plants get eaten up well before they get to flowering)

10. During Spring and Summer remember that plants need food too, just like people. Try a plant food such as **Yates Thrive Fish Blood & Bone** which has high levels of NPK nutrients for leafy plant growth.

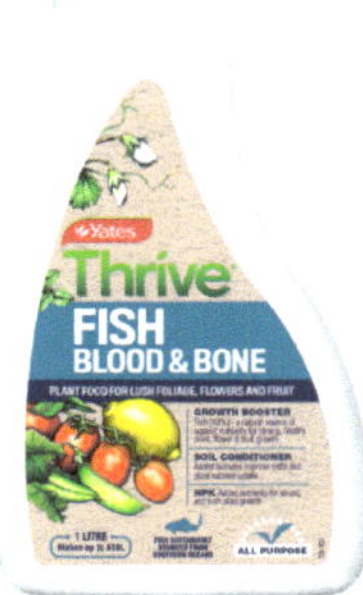

Handy Hint

If you are looking to encourage both caterpillars and butterflies into your garden, then **Yates Butterfly Field Seed Mix** is perfect. You can sprinkle it directly onto your garden bed – it has 33 different varieties of vibrant colourful plants that have nectar flowers to provide food for butterflies and feed and habitat for the caterpillars. It includes plants such as Swan Plant, Asclepias, Cosmos, Marigolds, Zinnia and Californian Poppy and many more.

Yates are proud to support the **BUTTERFLY MUSKETEERS WITH PROJECT SWAN PLANT** by donating 1000s of seeds to early childhood centres and schools to study the life cycle of a monarch butterfly in their classrooms.

Further Information

There are some amazing documentaries and shorter clips on the life cycle and mysteries of the monarch butterfly migration, caterpillars pupating, and monarchs emerging from chrysalises available on You Tube.

Keywords to type into You Tube include:
metamorphosis, caterpillar, monarchs,
monarch butterfly migration, monarch life cycle

Helpful websites:

www.thebutterflymusketeers.com

www.monarchwatch.org

www.monarch.org.nz

www.flightofthebutterflies.com

www.wikipedia.org/wiki/Danaus_plexippus

www.wikipedia.org/wiki/Asclepias

www.nationalgeographic.com

www.butterflyfunfacts.com

www.obsessionwithbutterflies.com

The science kit on the right is available
from all Whitcoulls stores for $25

A great group on Facebook is "*The Beautiful Monarch*" which has over 22,000 members and offers access to informative files, wonderful photos, interesting ideas, and advice on raising monarchs. If you have a question, it will be answered by other members in the group. This group was founded and created by the amazing Holli Webb Hearn.

www.facebook.com/butterflymusketeers

butterflymusketeers on Instagram

www.thebutterflymusketeers.com

Contact us
monarchs@thebutterflymusketeers.com

Butterfly life cycle word search answers

A word search puzzle grid:

N	E	C	T	A	R	T	N	M	M	E	G	G	K
D	W	T	Y	U	K	O	H	J	N	B	I	O	L
P	S	A	N	L	C	H	R	Y	S	A	L	I	S	S
U	A	S	Q	L	O	B	N	V	C	X	X	Z	A
P	S	D	W	M	I	G	R	A	T	I	N	G	Y
A	E	C	F	A	G	Y	U	I	O	O	P	H	M
U	E	A	T	L	N	S	S	A	A	F	L	O	E
L	M	T	R	L	S	P	D	A	S	C	I	J	T
O	E	E	E	I	Q	F	L	S	F	D	U	M	A
G	R	R	G	F	A	V	A	A	C	E	Y	H	M
D	G	P	K	E	D	B	R	S	N	A	Y	T	O
E	I	I	I	C	X	N	V	R	E	T	G	R	R
W	N	L	Y	Y	W	M	A	F	S	I	F	E	P
G	G	L	R	C	T	K	E	F	A	N	D	N	H
F	S	A	C	L	Y	O	P	C	F	G	S	Y	O
L	S	R	F	E	H	J	K	K	P	L	O	M	S
O	W	T	G	J	U	I	W	I	N	G	S	B	I
W	L	O	P	G	C	C	E	X	X	W	D	G	S
E	E	B	M	O	N	A	R	C	H	A	G	H	J
R	W	L	K	Q	R	R	H	Y	A	D	F	G	H
S	Y	U	J	G	B	U	T	T	E	R	F	L	Y
B	S	Z	A	S	T	O	P	C	K	A	S	W	T

Glossary

Abdomen - The black elongated hind part of the body, behind the thorax.

Antenna - (Plural, antennae) sense organ on an insect's head. Larval antennae are very small, while adult monarch butterfly ones are much longer.

Camouflage - A French word that means to hide or disguise. There are two types of camouflage: protective resemblance and protective coloration. Protective resemblance is when something looks like something else in its environment. Protective coloration is when something has the same colour or pattern as its surroundings.

Chrysalis - (Plural, chrysalises/chrysalides) another name for a butterfly pupa. That's the hard green casing that protects the caterpillar as it turns into a butterfly.

Cocoon - A silk web that encloses the pupae of many moths, but not butterflies.

Companion planting - Planting of different crops in close physical proximity, with the theory that they will help each other with aphids.

Cremaster - The posterior end of a pupa/chrysalis which contains hooks that fasten it to a pad of silk spun by the caterpillar.

Diapause - A period of reduced or halted development during any life stage. (Like the last generation of monarchs that migrate. Their sex organs are not fully developed. This is so they will mate at the end of migration).

Danaus plexippus - The scientific name of the monarch butterfly.

Entomologist - A scientist who studies insects. The study of insects is called entomology.

Eclosion - When a butterfly emerges from a chrysalis, or a caterpillar from an egg.

Exoskeleton - A hard skeleton located on the outside of an invertebrate's body (in contrast to the internal skeleton of vertebrates) that protects it and serves as a point for muscle attachment.

Forewing - Either one of the top two front wings on an insect with four wings.

Frass - The waste product of a caterpillar, called "caterpillar poop" by most students. Caterpillars produce a lot of this, especially in their later instars.

Hindwing - Either one of the two rear wings on an insect with four wings.

Inner margin - The trailing edge along the base of the wing.

Instar - A period between larval moults. There are five of these periods in the growth of a monarch larva.

Larva - (Plural, larvae) the second stage, after the egg, in metamorphosis. Also known as caterpillar.

Legs - Butterflies have six legs. These three pairs of legs are attached to the thorax, one pair in each segment of the thorax.

Life cycle - Butterflies go through four different life stages. An egg, larva (caterpillar), pupa,(chrysalis) and adult (monarch butterfly).

Migration - Movement of an organism or group from one habitat or location to another, usually periodic or seasonal movement of relatively long distance.

Moult - The process of shedding the skin or exoskeleton. Monarch larvae moult five times.

Overwintering - Also called hibernation, this is a condition in which an animal is dormant for a period of time.

Parasite - An organism (plant or animal) that lives on another organism (the host), obtaining nutrition from it and sapping or killing the host.

Pathogen - A bacterium, virus, or other micro organism that can cause disease.

Prolegs - Caterpillars have ten prolegs in total; eight abdomen prolegs and two anal prolegs.

Pheromones - Special chemicals released by some animals to communicate with other members of their species. They may be sensed over long distances and can help mates find each other. They may also help ensure that mating only occurs with other members of the same species.

Pollinator - An insect that carries pollen from flower to flower. Butterflies, moths and bees frequently do this.

Pollen - A fine powdery substance, consisting of microscopic grains discharged from the male part of a flower. The fertilising element of flowering plants, pollen is transported by the wind, insects, or other animals. Each grain contains a male gamete that can fertilise the female ovule.

Proboscis - Is the adult monarch's feeding tube, used for sucking nectar. The proboscis is coiled under the head when not in use.

Pupa - (Plural, pupae) is the third stage in metamorphosis, after the caterpillar stage. This is also termed as the non feeding stage. Commonly know as the chrysalis.

Pupate - To change from a larva (caterpillar) to a pupa (chrysalis).

Quasi extinction - Monarchs are at "substantial" risk of a quasi-extinction, which is when the population numbers become too low to rebound. This could happen over the next 20 years.

Scales - Overlapping pieces of chitin (the same material of which exoskeletons are made) that insulate butterflies' bodies and wings, improve their aerodynamics and give them colour and markings. Many people think the scales look like fine dust on butterfly wings. Please see the acknowledgement page for a close up photo of the scales.

Tagging - Is a process where a special numbered sticker is placed on the hindwing of the monarch butterfly. The number is entered into a database and if someone spots the butterfly and reports it, it give insight into the migration patterns of the monarch butterfly. Tagging can be done by anyone that is interested.

Warning coloration - Bright colours advertising poisons or other harmful defences to potential predators. Also called aposematic coloration.

We have only one planet, please treat it with love and respect, including all the people, animals and nature that share it with us. Everything on earth today is living and conscious. Each little thing you do can help to make the world a better planet for tomorrow. Be the difference.

www.ingramcontent.com/pod-product-compliance
Lightning Source LLC
Chambersburg PA
CBHW042117030726
47599CB00002B/247